A Marvelous Model of Ministry

A Message from the "Man in the Middle"

Roy Elton Brackins

MARVELOUS MODEL OF MINISTRY
PRINTED BY BOOKSURGE

Scripture taken from the New King James Version. Copyright © 1982 by Thomas Nelson, Inc. Used by permission. All rights reserved.

ISBN 1-4392-3248-2

Copyright © 2009 by Roy Elton Brackins

Printed in the United States of America
2009—First Edition

10 9 8 7 6 5 4 3 2 1

In memory of my parents, Mr. Leroy Brackins Jr.
and Mrs. Lucy Bell Brackins, who now sleep in the presence in Christ,
awaiting the great day when Jesus shall burst through the clouds
and the dead in Christ shall rise first—

No finer nor more godly people have I ever known in my life.
They epitomized lives of Christian character.

Also to my baby brother, Mr. Lionel Brackins,
who was blessed by God to have a voice
filled with glorious praise—
Rest on until the return of our Christ.

Contents

Foreword

T he Holy Scriptures readily establish the foundation, functionality, and fruit upon which every authentic servant of God may be recognized. Such servants are divinely appointed with passion, determinately active in their pursuit, and durably aggressive along the path to fulfilling the work that has been entrusted and assigned to their earthly tenure.

The distinctive qualities found in Moses as an Old Testament figure of a pastor are depicted in his assignment to deliver; and the qualities found in Joshua as an Old Testament figure of a leader are depicted in his assignment to lead. This truth affirms that servants are not established or evaluated by titles but by assignment.

In my humble estimation, the Spirit-filled pastor-teacher or godly leader is primarily positioned in ministry to exhibit and epitomize the heart of an authentic servant of God. The Lord expresses His intentions to provide loving reflections of Himself to His people through the unique and distinct personalities of pastors and leaders. To be certain, all leaders are not pastors, but every pastor is a leader.

The pastor-teacher is divinely released into the Body of Christ as an earthen vessel giving reverential stewardship to the entrustment of eternal treasures. In the fullness of God's assigned time these eternal treasures are sacredly distributed and deposited into the lives of others toward the ultimate accomplishment of progressive development.

When the Lord directed our lives to come together more than ten years ago, I could discern beyond all human denial that I had embraced the pleasure of meeting a man after God's own heart in the priceless personality of the author of this book, Pastor Roy Elton Brackins.

This book marks the initial deposit of God's glorious treasures that have been invested in him to be imparted into the heart of the servant-minded pastor or leader whose desire is to maximize ministry one aspect at a time.

The mindset of many modern-day pastors serving local churches of all sizes is confined to meeting the spiritual needs of people through the performance of preaching. The power of preaching is vital to the salvation of sinners and for the strength of the saints. However, the demands for meeting the practical needs of the saints that lie beyond the security of their salvation and strength necessitate pastoral and leadership initiatives that will deliver daily and long-term progressive results.

It is the sound conviction of the author to communicate the importance of meeting the holistic need of the Body of Christ by acknowledging the practicality of pastoral and leadership practices resulting in the accomplishment of life-changing encounters and experiences.

In a day when many pastors and leaders choose to measure their capacity to succeed by the success resulting from the purposeful potential of others, readers will be challenged to release their personal potential to excel and to succeed at levels of ministry they have never experienced before.

Pastors and leaders throughout every sect of the Body of Christ will benefit from the abundance of inspiration and instruction that are released and revealed in this book. Modeling ministry with a message, this book is sure to further the fruit of every servant of God in keeping with these words of the psalmist: "He shall be like a tree planted by the rivers of water, that bringeth forth his fruit in his season; his leaf also shall not wither; and whatsoever he doeth shall prosper."

A disciple in development,
S. L. Moton
Marlboro Heights Missionary Baptist Church
Killeen, Texas

Acknowledgments

I am grateful to God, His Son Jesus Christ, and the guidance of the Holy Spirit for using me to complete this volume, and I hope it will bless and encourage all who read it. In His mercy He has forgiven me, and in His grace He has showered me with the ability to accomplish what only He could do through me as I made myself totally available to Him. For this I am eternally grateful.

I thank God for my loving and supportive wife, Pamela, who has been a tremendous source of inspiration and encouragement. God has used her to see me through some of my darkest days, and we have enjoyed some of His most glorious sunrises of grace. You are truly my "grace gift" from God, and my "sweetie." I thank the Lord for our children: Ayonna Tywan, ArRhonda Camille, Laroya Trenise, and Montel Elton. God has used them to add such balance, peace, and purpose to my life. To my son-in-law, John, and the world's greatest grandchildren—Layla and Justine—I love you so very much.

I thank God for my siblings: Eleanor, who encouraged me; Jerri, who inspired me; Regina, who humored me; and Charles, who counseled me. God bless each of you just for being there when I needed you.

I thank God for my administrative assistants: Petrina Bonnick, Corsandra Graf, Peggy Peyton, and Beverly Williams. For all the typing, editing, reading, proofreading, and sending and receiving of emails, I say thank you and God bless you.

To the eleven full- and part-time staff members at the Grace Tabernacle Church, I say thank you for your unwavering commitment to excellence in ministry.

I thank God for some of the most precious people in the community of Christendom, the Grace Tabernacle Missionary Baptist Church family of Fort Worth, Texas. Thank you for all your prayers, encouragement, support, and the freedom—without chains or limitations—to be all God desires me to be.

I love each and every one of you with my *whole heart*.

Brother Roy

Introduction

A Message from the Man in the Middle

*T*his book is a brief compilation of better than thirty-six years of my life as a Christian, more than thirty-three years of preaching the gospel of Jesus Christ, and more than thirty years of leading God's people as a pastor. I was encouraged many years ago by my dear friend the Rev. David R. King, who now sleeps with the saints awaiting the resurrection, to write my first book. It was not until 2008 that God gave the go-ahead. I wanted this volume to be God glorifying, scripturally sound, saint strengthening, and a model of motivation for those who feel stuck at a level beneath their potential.

Perhaps you've attended conferences and seminars and heard stories of tremendous success. We've all heard about the churches that have grown from twenty-five to twenty-five hundred members—or even twenty-five thousand. We've heard about church school classes that have grown from four to eighty-four members. We know of musicians who started with twelve choir members, and now have four choirs with seventy-five members in each choir.

Often I left these conferences feeling discouraged, and I know I'm not alone in these thoughts. When these levels of growth do not take place in our ministries, discouragement and a sense of failure fill our minds. These stories of extraordinary and phenomenal growth are great testimonies to the grace of God, and I praise Him for these marvelous examples. But the reality is

God has chosen more of us to be connected to churches and ministries with fifty to a thousand members and Bible classes with five to twenty people. As a result of my experience, I asked the Lord to allow me to write a book to minister to what I call the "man (or ministry) in the middle."

I believe this resource is vitally important to help churches and ministries to transition from twenty members to two hundred, from forty to four hundred, in a healthy fashion. Many leaders are waiting on the fifteen thousand members and have failed to equip the seventeen, seventy-five or five hundred God has already trusted to their spiritual care. Also, many people are not more active in ministry because they do not consider themselves to be "superstars."

If you feel as though you have not reached the numerical levels you'd hoped for nor received all you desire in your ministry, you just may be a "man in the middle." If I've just described you, then I encourage you to keep reading. You're in good company, since that was the position Jesus purposefully chose to take.

At Calvary, He showed how a life totally surrendered to God can shine when He accepted His role as the ultimate "Man in the Middle." He was not crucified higher than those around Him. He was crucified beside them so He could reach them. Jesus embraced His role as the Middle Man because He knew God's best for His life was yet to come. The same is true for you and me.

I did not want this volume to be a collection of my personal opinions and ideologies. I wanted it to be based on the inerrant Word of God and filled with practical applications. Each chapter focuses on a passage of Scripture, and I hope and pray God will use what you receive to bless your life, ministry, and congregation as He tailors the information to fit your unique field of labor.

Be blessed and be a blessing.

Roy Elton Brackins

My Testimony

God's amazing grace. That phrase summarizes my life. I was born the third of four children in December 1955 to two of the most spiritually infused individuals I have ever known: Mr. and Mrs. Leroy Brackins Jr. All of us who grew up in that home in Houston, Texas, were not only taught Christian principles but saw those principles exemplified in our parents every day. They not only took us to church, they also taught us the importance of the Bible. In addition, they demonstrated forgiveness and love to us and to each other, shaping our character in ways that remain with us to this very day.

Our home was always filled with people, prayer, and praise. I can remember how we children were commanded to gather around the piano. We would sing gospel music until we could feel the presence of God in our living room. Even though we did not realize the profundity of those times, they left a positive and indelible imprint on our spiritual growth that still resonates in our souls.

At the age of twelve, I developed a fondness for the guitar and convinced (so I thought) my father to loan me the money to purchase my first electric guitar for twelve dollars. He challenged me to learn to play it in a month. If I did, I would not have to pay back the loan. Thank God I learned to play four songs in two weeks!

At fifteen, I decided to try my hand at the piano. By that time I knew the keys and scale well enough to transpose the guitar notes and correlate them with the notes on the piano. With the help of my father, who was a musician, and my oldest sister, I eventually learned both piano and organ.

In junior high and high school, I used my musical gifts to play in several rock and roll bands. Unfortunately, this also led me into environments that were polluted with drugs and ungodly behavior. During this time, I chose to neglect and ignore the sound biblical principles and Christian teachings my parents had instilled in me. Between the ages of fifteen and fifteen days before my eighteenth birthday, I was deceived by the devil into leading a secret life of drug abuse. But on December 6, 1973, I was confronted by the life-changing, soul-saving power of Jesus Christ.

I tell people it happened something like this: The Holy Spirit caught a ship across the Mediterranean Sea and kept right on going across the Atlantic Ocean. He got off the ship in Florida, rented a car, and headed through Alabama, Mississippi, and Louisiana. When He got to Texas, He drove down to Houston and got on the 610 freeway. He got off at North Main Street, made a right-hand turn onto 41st Street, and drove until He arrived at 721 East 41st Street. He walked into my parents' home without even knocking on the door. He walked past my mother and father because He already owned them. He walked past my sisters because He owned them as well. He stopped right at the piano, where I was sitting on the little round stool. My sinful behavior had led me to be strung out on drugs, and I was exhausted. But when I heard Him calling me to surrender my life, I could not deny or escape His voice. I accepted Jesus as my Savior and Lord about 4:30 that afternoon.

The next day at school I shared with my friends the positive change Jesus had made in my life. Some of them accepted it and others rejected it, but that did not prevent me from walking in His grace and sharing my story. I never returned to the bondage of illegal drug abuse again.

After my conversion experience, I began to use my musical gifts in a positive way at local churches in my community: True Light Baptist,

Bethlehem Baptist, Green Chapel A.M.E., and Mount Pilgrim Baptist. I also joined a Christian band and recorded my first record, a song I wrote and produced titled "Believer."

Nearly three years later, in August of 1976, the Lord called me into the gospel ministry at the age of twenty. I had no formal college training then and still do not. But by His grace God assigned me to my first pastorate in Chappell Hill, Texas, at the Ebenezer Baptist Church in 1979. I served there until April 1982, and from there He assigned me to the Pleasant Grove Baptist Church in College Station, Texas. In June of 1983, He challenged me to accept the call to lead the Glen Park Baptist Church in Fort Worth. I remained there until April of 1987, when the Lord led me to organize the Grace Tabernacle Baptist Church in May of that same year.

My journey has been one of faith, trust, total dependence, and confidence in God. Many times I did not understand why God was allowing what He was allowing, but my faith in Him was never shattered.

In the early days, our church worshipped in our home and in hotels, and we baptized new believers in hotel swimming pools.

Since then, the Lord has allowed me to lead His people into purchasing a church home (1993), remodeling that facility (2002), and building a children and youth center (2003). Then from 2005 to 2007, we watched God open the door for the completion of phases one and two of our present church campus. Grace Tabernacle now rests on six acres and includes a 550-seat sanctuary, classrooms, nursery, fellowship hall, kitchen, children's playground area, and five administrative offices. We have grown from twenty-seven members with two ministries to better than five hundred members with thirty-five active, vibrant, and need-meeting ministries.

The Lord decided to rescue a rusty-kneed boy from the Studewood community of Houston and give him the responsibility of leading His people. My life is proof positive that God is not looking for people with ability, but for people who will surrender to Him their availability. He has forgiven me of my sins, written my name in the Lamb's book of life, and placed the joy of working for Him in my soul.

God has taught me to use to the fullest what He's given me. I have made a conscious decision not to complain or question Him about those gifts and resources He has not showered me with. Instead, I choose to utilize to His glory those things He has placed at my disposal. Many of the details of my ecclesiastical expedition are discussed in various chapters throughout this volume. I hope this testimony encourages you and opens the door for you to experience the peace and grace available to those who walk with, live in, and work for Jesus Christ.

Wherever you are in your ministry, always keep this truth in mind: God is able to do exceedingly and abundantly above all that we can ask, dream, desire, or imagine. He may not do it today or tomorrow, but as long as we live, He still has work for us to accomplish, and He will give us the strength and ability to get the job done.

2

Prayer, the Personal Touch

Praying always with all prayer and supplication in the Spirit,
being watchful to this end with all perseverance and supplication
for all the saints.

EPHESIANS 6:18

One of the many things I have discovered as a believer in Jesus Christ is the power of consistent and devoted prayer. It is through prayer that we are able to

- establish our connection to God;
- exhibit our care for other believers in the body of Christ; and
- epitomize our commitment to the work of the kingdom.

We establish our connection to God not just through daily but through all-day devotions and conversations with Him. We not only talk to Him, we also listen as He speaks to us with words of comfort and reassurance.

We exhibit our care for other members of the body of Christ as we take their petitions to the Lord and partner with them in prayer. The best way to take your attention away from your problems is to pray with someone else about their problems.

We then epitomize our commitment to the work of the kingdom by remaining consistent in our prayer lives. All the work of God is fueled by His power as we petition Him in prayer. Prayer is our motivational force that sustains us in the mammoth fights we face in ministry faithfulness. It is through prayer that we seek God's will, hear His voice, and follow His direction. Many believers fail to realize the power and the purpose Jesus had in mind when He gave us the command to pray. It is not an option but a vital and fundamental factor that will determine the depth of our relationship with God and our loyalty to His call upon our lives.

Some say they sit idly in church because they are not aware of God's purpose for their lives. My response to them has always been, "You will never discover God's purpose without consistent communication with Him."

In his letter to the Ephesian church, Paul shared principles of prayer that are still relevant and important to our bond with our heavenly Father through His Son Jesus Christ. He tells us to pray "always with all prayer and supplication in the Spirit" (6:18). This verse helped to revolutionize my prayer life when I understood and applied the principles found there.

I have discovered five important aspects of prayer that enhance the ease and level of inclusion God desires us to have in our times of communication with Him. Let's look at all five individually.

1. Adoration

Many of us begin our prayer time begging and making requests of God. We fail to realize how important it is for us to reverence who He is before we ask Him for what we think we need. When we spend time in adoration, both our prayer lives and our worship will improve. Adoration teaches us how to honor God just for who He is. If He never does anything for us, He is still completely and perfectly holy and supremely sovereign. Ask yourself, "How long would a relationship last between a friend and me if that person asked me for something every time he or she talked or communicated with me?" Now, "When was the last time you talked to God without asking Him for something?" Answering these questions helps us put into proper perspective the need to honor, adore, reverence, and esteem God before we present our requests.

David said in Psalm 34:1, "I will bless the Lord at all times; His praise shall continually be in my mouth." I have also discovered that when I begin my prayer time with adoration, I realize that what I thought was important to say to Him was not nearly as important as what He wanted to say to me!

Our private worship of God helps us to make right requests of God. The more time we spend in His presence, the better able we are to discover those things He desires to do through us, for us, and with us.

As we seek to expand our prayer lives in the area of adoration, I have also found it helpful to remember some of the many names God was given throughout His word.

JEHOVAH JIREH

He is **Jehovah Jireh**, the God who provides. Everything we have has come from His hand, and whatever we need is in His hand. I'd like to elaborate here, because many people make the drastic mistake of abandoning their relationship with God when they are going through difficult financial times.

After Job lost his children and everything he owned, he made an amazing statement of faith: "The Lord gives and the Lord takes away." Job was not about to abandon God, because he knew all he once had had come from the hand of God, and he had a much better chance of receiving it back from God by remaining close to Him.

> **If God provided for us in the past, He is able to do it again, but we must remain closely connected to Him.**

JEHOVAH RAPHA

He is **Jehovah Rapha**, the God who heals. Even if you are experiencing pain in your body, His promise of everlasting health will far outweigh the temporary pain. Our bodies are impermanent and susceptible to infection and disease. But we know that Christ's work at Calvary has provided for us new bodies that will never experience pain or sickness.

SHEPHERD

He is our **Shepherd**, who guides us through difficult and uncertain circumstances. We never travel alone; He is always with us even when we are not aware of His presence. Take a moment to reflect on one of the lowest and most difficult periods in your life. What you may not have grasped is that the only way you were able to make it through that season was because He kept you while you were in it. After His maturing process was complete, He led you out of the darkness, and He remains with you at this present moment.

IMMANUEL

Above all these, we can adore Him because He is **Immanuel**, God with us.

> **God loved us to the degree that He was willing
> to reduce Himself to human flesh, and immortality
> became mortal so we could see His love in action.
> God came to our neighborhood.**

We live in cities that have some unfavorable areas. But when Jesus came to earth, He did not seclude Himself. Rather He chose to mingle with us, walk with us, attend our wedding feasts, and transform our funerals into family reunions.

When we understand these names of God and utilize these principles in the adoration portion of our prayer lives, we will see our times of communion with God revolutionized.

2. CONFESSION

God wants our lives to be free from all unconfessed sin. To confess means to acknowledge. Often, we overlook the need to acknowledge our sins by name when we confess them to Him. How many times have we said, "Lord, I ask You to forgive my sins, in Jesus' name, amen," and left it there? Naming our sins is important because it helps us to see sin from God's perspective.

An incident with my wife and our son really brought this principle to light for me. When he was younger, Montel got in trouble in school one day. When he and his mother arrived home, I was in the den watching television. She walked in with him and said, "Go tell your daddy what you did at school."

"Daddy, I got in trouble at school."

My wife said, "No! Tell him what you did."

Montel began to cry and began to name the trouble item by item. After he finished I asked him if it bothered him to have to confess those things to me.

"Yes sir."

"The only way you will never have to confess those things to me again is to never do them again."

Likewise, God wants us to know He expects our confession of sin to bring pain and embarrassment to our hearts so that we will repent and be determine not to commit those acts again. Then, as with my son, we will never have to confess them again.

Unconfessed sin in the life of a believer should cause uneasiness. It hinders and stagnates our closeness with God. But 1 John 1:9 says, "If we confess our sins, He is faithful and just to forgive us our sins and to cleanse us from all unrighteousness."

Confession teaches us how to view sin from God's perspective, and if we truly love Him we will avoid those things that bring pain and displeasure to His heart.

3. THANKSGIVING

Another important element of prayer is thanksgiving. When we take time to think about all God has done for us, as well as all He has kept from us, we could thank Him for days.

Often when I walk in my neighborhood for exercise I use that time for prayer. Here are a few things I thank God for as I walk. Perhaps my list will prompt you in your times of thanksgiving.

- I thank God for my legs, my feet, and the tennis shoes I wear.
- I thank Him for my sweat socks and for the blessing of having dress socks to change into after my walk is completed.
- I thank Him for my neighborhood, the home I just left, and the joy of being able to return to it.
- I thank Him for my eyes to see where I am walking.
- I thank Him for protecting me from traffic.
- I thank Him for the oxygen in my lungs, the blood in my veins, and the strength in my body.

I think you get the picture. Amazingly, these words of thanksgiving are only about my morning walk. It has been said, "We must think about God more in order to thank Him properly." When we employ thanksgiving into our prayer lives, we will realize we are blessed beyond measure, and no matter what we are growing through, life could be a whole lot worse.

> We need to learn how to cancel our complaint campaigns and adapt a disposition of genuine gratitude. Very seldom do we stop and ask ourselves, "How successful has my complaining been, and what matters have been resolved because of it?"

There is an amazing lesson to be gleaned from Luke 11:1. Jesus called His disciples in Luke 5–6. He gave them power and authority to preach and heal in Luke 9. They, however, did not come to understand what they really needed until Luke 11. There they asked the Lord to teach them to pray.

They did not mind admitting to their incompetence in this area, and perhaps we could learn something from them. We need to ask ourselves, "Is it possible we are so powerless and so easily defeated by the devil because we don't know how to pray and our pride will not allow us to ask someone to teach us?"

Thanksgiving helps to move our attention from what we want from God to being grateful for all He has already done.

4. SUPPLICATION

Supplication is asking God to meet our specific needs. On a list of five it is next to last, but most of us place it first. When Jesus taught His disciples to pray, He told them to ask God, "Give us day by day our daily bread" (Luke 11:3). I believe the main reason He taught us to pray like this was to save us from unnecessary anxiety. Most of our worries and concerns are related to things that have not even happened yet. When we learn to ask God to meet our needs on a day-by-day basis, then trust Him to do so, a great deal of stress will automatically be removed from our lives. Many of us have concerns about next week, next month, and even next year, but Jesus said worrying will not alter the outcome. We do not pray in an attempt to change God's mind. Instead, we pray to do three basic things:

1. to discover God's will for our lives;
2. to display His will through our lives;
3. to keep from deviating from His will with our lives.

Our supplications should always be God-centered. By this I mean they should always have God's glory in mind. Why should God grant our requests if He is not going to be glorified through the answer? Why should God give us a car we will drive everywhere but to His house? Why should God give us a job that will cause us to be too tired or too busy to worship Him? Our supplications should be about seeking the heart of God and not the hand of God.

Besides glorifying God with our requests, we must also keep in mind our relationship with Him. The more we realize our need for God, the more we talk to Him and depend on Him. When He provides for us one day at a time, we are forced to go back to Him for the next day's needs. God wants to talk to us regularly because He loves us so much. He also knows that if He gives us too much at one time, we will likely abandon Him and not return until we exhaust all of His resources.

As we seek to develop healthy prayer lives, we must include adoration, confession, thanksgiving, supplication, and intercession.

5. INTERCESSION

We are responsible to pray for one another. Paul says in Ephesians 6:18, "...with all perseverance and supplication for all the saints." Then in verse 19 he asks them to pray that he might "open [his] mouth boldly to make known the mystery of the gospel." I often ask those in leadership at the Grace Tabernacle Church the following question: "How effective would my preaching and teaching be if I were totally dependent on your prayers as the source of my power?"

Most of us want to be connected to churches with powerful preaching, praise, teaching, excellent ministries, and great outreach programs. Yet we fail to intercede for those who lead and work in those ministries.

In our church we have a "Tribe Ministry." Their role is to make sure every member of the family of Grace Tabernacle is covered with prayer at least once a week with a call or a personal visit. (I will say more about this ministry in a later chapter.) People are hurting, they need to know someone cares about them, and there is no better way to show the love of Jesus than through the power of intercessory prayer.

Many people say they don't pray in public because they are ashamed. The principle we must consider in this area is twofold. First, God is our heavenly Father, and He hears everything we say to Him from the genuineness of our hearts. Second, how would you feel if one of your friends never spoke to you or even acknowledged your presence in public, but only behind closed doors? When we pray, we are not talking to people, we are talking to our heavenly Father.

Recently I called from my cell phone to pray for one of my friends. He later told me the connection was bad and he did not hear all of the prayer because the call dropped. I replied, "Don't worry about it. The One I was praying to heard the entire petition. I was praying for you, but praying to Him."

We must direct our petitions to heaven without concerning ourselves with meeting the expectations of other people.

> **When we include these five aspects in all of our prayers, we will discover the time we spend with God will increase, and the joy we experience with Him will transcend our greatest expectations.**

God does not always answer our prayers to our satisfaction, but He does reveal His perfect will if we will be persistent and patient.

A WORD FOR PASTORS AND LEADERS

Grace Tabernacle's hands-on approach to prayer has been extremely beneficial to the ministries, growth, and development in our church. If you do not do so already, begin praying each week for the leadership in your church. Follow that up by encouraging leaders to pray for those who work with them in specific areas of ministry. You will be amazed at the number of conflicts, failures, and frustrations that dissipate just because you took those matters of concern to God before you attempted to resolve them on your own.

3

The Importance of Worship and Praise

Enter into His gates with thanksgiving,
And into His courts with praise.
Be thankful to Him, and bless His name.
PSALM 100:4

In chapter 2, we examined the significance of our private prayer time with God. In this chapter our focus will be on the public praise we offer to God. I believe worship and praise are two of the most powerful weapons God has made available to every one of His children. And, using these weapons requires no previous education or experience. All we need is oxygen. Now that may sound strange, but I make this statement based on the Word of God. Psalm 150:6 commands, "Let everything that has breath praise the Lord!" We may not have much money, perfect health, secure jobs, or problem-free relationships, but if we are breathing (and the very fact that you are reading this book is a good sign that you are), we have a God-given command and responsibility to praise the Lord!

Before we look at some very important principles of praise, allow me to dismiss some misconceptions and erroneous propaganda about true worship and praise.

MISCONCEPTIONS REGARDING PRAISE AND WORSHIP

First, praise should never be offered to impress those around us, but rather to please the heart of our heavenly Father. Praise should not be dictated by our circumstances.

> As believers in Jesus Christ we are to be thermostats and not thermometers. Thermostats control the temperature, while thermometers are forced to adjust to the temperature around them.

Second, praise should not require any prompting or manipulation. Our very presence in a worship experience should cause the warmth of the Holy Spirit's presence to be felt by all those who are around us. God loves truly spontaneous praise. Now, I am not suggesting that the role of worship and praise leaders is not a vital and significant part of the worship experience. We must understand, however, that their role is to lead us into praise, to usher us into the atmosphere of praise, and not to coerce or pressure us into praise. Praise must begin in our hearts before we ever express it with our hands and voices. As with our prayer lives, praise must include private preparation.

Third, our worship should not be based on what God has done for us (I will address that under the umbrella of praise), but on who He is. He is the Creator of all things, the totality of all that is tangible. He is the sovereign God who relies on no one but Himself. He is from everlasting to everlasting, and He is always coming to where He is coming from. He is the epitome of love and grace personified in His Son Jesus Christ.

Our worship of God and our praise to God really have two different dimensions, which we'll look at in the following pages.

WORSHIP

Some people struggle with worship because they believe God must do something for us before we offer Him our true worship.

If you're a sports fan, think for a moment about your favorite team. (If you're not a sports fan, think about your friend's or spouse's favorite team.) Why do you cheer, clap, and scream for them? Because they do what they do so well, right? Now, has this team ever done anything for you personally? Of course not. We cheer for our favorite teams, not because of what they've done for us, but because of what they are able to do.

Sports personalities and entertainment figures have "fading fame." But Jesus remains the same yesterday, today, and forevermore. Therefore, even if you do not think God has done enough for you, you can still worship Him because of what He is able to do. For example,

- Maybe He has not healed your body, but He is able to heal. He healed a woman who suffered for twelve years with an issue of blood. Worship Him for that.
- Maybe He has not given you a promotion on your job, but He is able to promote. He promoted David from leading sheep in his father's backyard to leading the entire nation of Israel. Worship Him for that.
- Maybe He has not given you a child, but He is able to open barren wombs. He heard Hannah's prayer and blessed her with a son after many years of barrenness. Worship Him for that.

Worship is not about what God has done for us; it is about what God is able to do.

> The Hebrew boys said to King Nebuchadnezzar, "Our God may not deliver us from the fiery furnace, but we want you to know that we know He is able."

Just because God does not answer our request in the manner we think He should does not mean that He is unable to do so. I have lived long enough to learn that God does not shelter me from every storm, but He allows my worship to develop right in the midst of them. Our worship will very often dictate our deliverance.

PRAISE

Praise is a close relative of worship, but the two are not the same. We worship because of who God is. We praise God in recognition of all He has done for us. Praise is just our way of regularly saying to God, "Thank You for all You have done."

We express our gratitude by lifting of hands, shouts of praise, tears of joy, or even with the dance of exaltation. In my estimation this should be one of the primary components in the life of a Christian. We tell our children (or we were taught as children) to say thank you whenever someone does something nice for them or gives them something. God blesses us continuously, so for the child of God praise should be as regular as breathing is.

Another misconception about worship and praise lies in the belief that the number of people present in a worship experience determines the level and authenticity of the praise. Many worship leaders and musicians have not made themselves totally available to God because they feel as though the field where God has planted them is too sparse.

Understand it is not the size of your praise that gets God's attention; it is the substance of your praise that brings joy to God's heart and glory to His name. The Bible teaches us that God inhabits the praise of His people. Whenever a group gathers with the exclusive intent of worshipping God and praising His name for the wonderful things He has done, we can always rest assured of His presence.

There is also another serious hindrance which prohibits us from experiencing the true joy of worship and praise. I call it "entrance distraction."

David said in Psalm 100:4, "Enter into His gates with thanksgiving, and into His courts with praise. Be thankful to Him, and bless His name." Have you ever thought about how most of us enter the house of the Lord? I contend that the manner in which we enter His house will determine the genuineness we exhibit while we are there. Consider this: Would you be offended if someone came to your home and spoke to other people who were there and never even acknowledged your presence? When was the last time you entered the house of God and spoke to Him before you talked with other people? If we would be offended by this behavior, we need to know that God is also.

Often our worship is not genuine because we have allowed other people to distract us before we enter into God's presence. I try to whisper a word of prayer each time I enter any church. This helps me keep my focus on who I am there to hear from and to give glory to.

David said we should enter God's house with thanksgiving. We should make our arrival with a posture of praise. We should not wait until we are comfortable in our pews or emotionally stirred by the singing of choirs or the ornate trappings of the place we worship. We should arrive with hearts filled with gratitude, minds inculcated with appreciation, and hearts running over with abundant veneration.

During times of our public worship and praise we must keep in mind at least two things: the owner of the house we are entering and the reason we are there.

> **We enter *His* gates! We come into *His* courts, and we should do both of them with *praise*!**

The gates of Psalm 100 represent what we would call a "vestibule." This is where we should clear our minds of any and all worldly concerns. We must consciously recognize that we are about to enter into the presence of the holy and Most High God. We would not hesitate to carefully prepare to meet and be in the presence of the president of the United States or the queen of England. But how many of us make the necessary spiritual preparations to stand, sit, or bow in the presence of the Creator of the universe? Presidents change every four or eight years, kings and queens change every generation, but God has remained on His throne from eternity. Enter His gates. Arrive with appreciation. Leave your cares and agendas outside.

> **When our hearts are filled with worship and praise, we have no room left to carry anything else.**

After we arrive with appreciation, we then have the responsibility to activate our adoration. When we experience difficulties of some sort prior to our arrival at the house of the Lord, as most of us have, we usually find that our praise does not come on automatically. We have to activate it. The best way to do this is to think about His goodness. We must never allow our burdens to blind us from the blessing found in praising God. When our minds think about His goodness, then our mouths should express our gratefulness.

> **Whatever God has done for us is more than we deserve; and whatever difficulties God has allowed are far less than we deserve. This truth alone should cause us to give God unqualified praise.**

Now that we've looked at several misconceptions, let's consider some very important components to authentic worship and praise.

PREPARATION FOR PRAISE

I have often wondered how powerful our praise to God would be if every minister of music, every musician, and every director prayed each week for all their choir personnel name by name. I also wonder how much more effective the minister of music, musicians, and directors would be if every person who is a part of that ministry would pray for them. I believe the real preparation for praise does not begin in rehearsal, but in our secret closets and places of prayer.

Often we arrive at rehearsals and to worship with the cares of this world on our minds. We fail to ask God for a spirit of cooperation and unity. More often than not, we just jump right into rehearsing and wonder why our music ministries seem to be overwhelmed with problems and turnover in leadership.

We must not view the act of praise as a job. I get really annoyed (pray for me, please) when people refer to their work as a church musician or director as a "gig." The word *gig* means a performance, appearance, or a show. That is not worship, it is entertainment. If God has gifted you with musical talent, don't take it lightly. Instead, use it properly for His glory. The best way to accomplish this is to prepare appropriately. We must ask Him to free our minds and work through us so we might bless the body of Christ.

PARTICIPATION IN PRAISE

Most football games include cheerleaders. Those jumping, yelling pom-pom waving individuals whose job is to pump up the crowd, motivate excitement, and encourage everyone to make noise and root for the team. I am always amazed, however, by the true fans in the stands who really love their team. When they are present, you can hardly hear a word the cheer-leaders are saying because the crowd always drowns them out. This principle seems to work in every venue except the church.

We know the worship leader and musicians are responsible to lead us in praise, but they should not have to do it alone. Psalm 34:1, 3 really helps in placing this matter in its proper perspective. David begins by saying, "I will bless the Lord at all times; His praise shall continually be in my mouth." But by the time he reaches verse 3 he says, "Oh, magnify the Lord with me, and let us exalt His name together." Within three verses he transitions from a solo to a symphony. There is no greater thrill than to be in worship when all the people of God are participating in genuine, unrestrained, God-centered praise. God wants each voice to be a part of the symphony of praise we offer to Him. He wants to hear that perfect sound, that sound that expresses true praise.

THE PORTABILITY OF PRAISE

We need to learn how to carry the praise of God with us from His house back to our homes. We need God's manifested presence in our living rooms as much as in His sanctuary. God's presence can impact our offices and cubicles throughout the week just like it impacts the pulpits on Sundays. God's presence can impact our cars in the same way it impacts the choir lofts. We need praise to be a part of our daily activity and not limited to a thirty-minute Sunday morning session. We do not need choirs, musicians, directors, or even a pastor to usher us into the atmosphere of God's presence. All we need is a mind to think about His goodness, grace, guidance, and glory, and we can transform our present environment into a place of wondrous worship and panacean praise. When we carry worship and praise with us, worship and praise will carry us through some circumstances we could never face alone. Again, your praise could very well determine your deliverance.

My challenge to you is to strive to become a genuine representative to those around you of what true praise and its impact is all about. Take some time each day to read a psalm, sing a favorite hymn or song, and reverently worship God in private and you will discover what a great impact it will have on your public praise.

A WORD FOR PASTORS AND LEADERS

Most pastors find the tardiness of those who populate the pew annoying. Often we wonder, "Why do they always arrive after the worship has begun?" I think a good place to find an answer to this question is in the mirror. How visible and vibrant are you during the worship and praise period or the devotional time at your church? Often members do not see us present in the sanctuary or participating, and they conclude, "If it is not important enough for my pastor or leader to be involved, why should I be involved?" As leaders we must set the pace and the example in worship that we desire others to follow. In 1 Samuel 6:14-22, we read how King David set the example for praise by dancing before the Lord with all his might. As a result, the maidservants held him in honor and esteem. Your example could very well help another bashful or young convert to Christ discover how important the components of worship and praise are to the development of a child of God.

4

No Need for a Second Opinion

But when it pleased God, who separated me from my mother's womb and called me through His grace to reveal His Son in me, that I might preach Him among the Gentiles, I did not immediately confer with flesh and blood.
GALATIANS 1:15–16

One of life's most disheartening experiences has to be receiving bad news from the doctor. Many people have heard their medical professionals recommend surgery, when they were hoping to hear "All is well." Others have been told they only have a few months to live, or that a dramatic change in their lifestyles and diets must occur. Many years ago we were forced to accept the recommendations of the one doctor we visited because we had no other options. Now, however, after receiving a gloomy and dreary report, we can seek a second opinion before we make any major health decisions.

History has proven that second opinions can be extremely valuable. Second opinions have caused surgical recommendations to become only medication changes. Second opinions have canceled cancer threats. Second opinions have revealed that the growth was not a tumor, only a cyst. Second opinions have calmed hearts, relieved fearful minds, renewed passions for continued living, and prevented many unnecessary procedures. Second opinions are indeed worth pursuing when a human being gives the first opinion. But when God speaks, it is final, thorough, complete, undebatable—and there is no need for a second opinion.

Here's why. When one physician gives a prognosis, he or she may be unaware of the latest technological or pharmaceutical advancements or discoveries. So a patient seeks a second opinion in hopes that the next doctor will be more knowledgeable and will have been exposed to more than the first person. With God, however, there are no new discoveries, advancements, or procedures. He created everything, knows everything, and all wisdom comes from Him. His thoughts and ways are beyond finding out. Isaiah 55:8–9 says, "'For My thoughts are not your thoughts, nor are your ways My ways,' says the Lord. 'For as the heavens are higher than the earth, so are My ways higher than your ways, and My thoughts than your thoughts.'" This helps us understand that when God speaks, we don't need to consult any person, place, or thing for a second opinion!

In Galatians 1, Paul gives a capsulized report of his conversion experience. On the Damascus road, while on his way to persecute the church, he met the master, miraculous, magnificent, molder of mercies, the matchless Lamb of God. On that day Paul was knocked off his beast, and while lying flat on his back he looked up and met Jesus. He was instantly transformed by the quickening power of Jesus Christ of Calvary. After this encounter he was sent to the home of a man named Judas. He spent three days there without eating or seeing. When the time was right the Lord sent a man named Ananias to him to lay hands on him, and the Bible says scale-like objects fell from his eyes, he received the Holy Spirit, and was baptized after Ananias prayed for him.

Here in the book of Galatians Paul goes to some extremes to emphasize the genuineness of his *calling*, his *commission*, and his *confidence*, which were exclusively in God through Jesus Christ. I believe Paul shared this because he wanted to warn us of the danger of discussing with other people whether we should or should not do what God has called and commanded us to do. Notice how he begins verse 15: "But when it pleased God." As children of God we should never seek second human opinions, even from well-intentioned people because it compromises the delight of God in our lives.

COMPROMISING GOD'S DELIGHT

Paul says, "But when it pleased God." We must never seek to please ourselves with any decisions or actions that displease God. This word *pleased* literally means God thought well of Paul in spite of his past hideous malefactions and gross antipathies. God was pleased with Paul not because of what he had done in the past, but in spite of what he had done in the past. I believe Paul was able to say "it pleased God" because Jesus had made personal contact with his life. He had been touched by the Master. God has the ability to change, reshape, and redirect our lives, then get pleasure out of using us to His glory. God is always pleased when we cooperate and surrender to His will. However, when we choose to discuss or debate with others that which we know God has called us to do, we compromise His delight in us.

Our disobedience or inactivity breaks God's heart! And He has been too good to us for us to break His heart. We need to answer one paramount question as we strive to make decisions after we have heard His voice: Will God be pleased with my final decision?

Many of us make the mistake of seeking only to please ourselves, and we give very little attention to pleasing God. When we choose to sit on the sidelines, knowing we could make a difference in helping our churches grow, God is not pleased. When we listen to a second opinion, we run the risk of breaking God's heart by compromising His delight. God wants to be pleased with our lives.

Paul also says in this verse, "...who separated me from my mother's womb and called me through His grace." He knew there was no need for a second opinion because it could have crippled God's design for his life.

CRIPPLING GOD'S DESIGN

Notice he says, "God separated me," speaking of his conversion experience. He also says, "God called me," referring to his commission assignment. Paul is sharing with us the dual nature of his task from God. His life included both salvation and service. He was willing to prepare himself so that neither his salvation nor his service would be crippled by his failure to cooperate with God's plan for his life.

When Paul says he was separated from his mother's womb, he means he had come to recognize that what he was now doing was what God had planned for his life since the very day of his birth. Paul also knew that God will not force His children into His service. He will do whatever is necessary to get our attention, but He will not violate His established boundary whereby He allows us choose to follow Him, work for Him, and live for Him. When we look closely at the syntax and grammatical arrangement of this verse, the Holy Spirit allows us to make an amazing discovery about the word *separated*. This word as it is used here has at least two definitions. One is to be detached from something or someone. The other is to be used exclusively for the glory of something or someone. This helps greatly in understanding why many of us have crippled God's design for our lives. We are still *attached* to some things God wants us to be free from, and we are still *detached* from some things God wants us to be connected to.

Whenever our attachments and detachments are out of kilter, the result will always be a crippled lifestyle. Paul is letting us know that if we are going to fulfill our calling by faith through God's grace, we must release those things that displease Him and hold tightly to those things that honor

Him. Part of this process included ignoring any person or group who gives us advice that does not strictly coincide with the Word of God. We need to detach ourselves from people who are biblically illiterate and attach ourselves to people who are grounded in God's Word.

Now, I am not suggesting that we cut off all communication and association with those who are not stable in the Word of God. However, we must not depend on them for advice on spiritual matters. Likewise, we cannot help them to grow in Christ properly if our relationship with Him is unstable. Whenever we are attached to the wrong things, we will automatically be detached from the right things.

Another way in which Paul was separated from his mother's womb had to do with his heritage. Paul was raised in a strictly orthodox Jewish home and skilled in the law by his parents and his teachers. The orthodox Jews did not believe Jesus was the Christ. But when Paul met Jesus, he perhaps had to tell his parents and other relatives he would no longer be able to deny what he knew to be the undisputable truth about the incarnation of God.

Very often the flesh will lead us to do one thing even though God's Word says something diametrically opposite. When we fail to obey God's Word, we cripple God's design for our lives. We may have home issues, personal issues, disposition issues, emotional issues, and even pride issues that cripple us. Whatever they may be, our challenge is to say no to our flesh and yes to the will of God.

> **God's purpose will not lead us any further
> than His grace is able to keep us.**

CLOUDING GOD'S DISPLAY

We can glean another important principle from this passage. Paul wrote in verse 16, "To reveal His Son in me, that I might preach Him among the

Gentiles." I believe this was his way of informing us about his determination not to cloud God's display through his life.

Many people have a distorted image of Christ because we have offered a cloudy presentation of Him. Paul tells us he had been called by God for the exclusive purpose of revealing Jesus Christ to the Gentiles. The word *reveal* means God was able to present Jesus with crystal clarity to the Gentiles through the apostle Paul.

I believe a cloudy display of Christ includes an unstable faith, a lack of commitment, inconsistent enthusiasm, and unpredictable dedication. It is only when the will of God and the person of Christ become clear to us that we are able to present Him clearly to others.

Whenever God's Word gives clear direction, and we consult an unsaved, unscriptural, or even well-intentioned person for advice, hoping to contradict the Bible, we are polluting our minds with ungodly foreign substances. There's nothing wrong with asking for advice, but it must include wise counsel and sound biblical guidance. We must seek advice from other Spirit-filled people who will help us accomplish what we know God has called us to do. If God is calling you to a teaching ministry, don't ask another person whether you should teach. Instead, seek out those who already excel in that area so they can inspire you to develop into the best vessel God can use.

When God called me to preach, I was not what some would call "educationally prepared." On a scale of one to ten, my public articulation and communication skills were about a two. I was a young convert, saved by His grace from drug addiction and hideous behavior. After my conversion I had a wife and two small children, very little money to pay the bills, and no money to enroll in college. But I knew what God had called me to do. I did not consult anyone about my ineptness or insufficiencies; I chose rather to place myself in the company of men and women who were being greatly used by God. One of my sisters, Jerri, helped me with my articulation skills. My oldest sister, Eleanor, helped me develop my worship and praise skills, and my parents supported me greatly with their encouraging words and constant presence. God exposed me to many mentors in ministry: Dr. William Bowie Jr., George Curry Sr., and Melvin Wade Sr., to name a few. All of these individuals helped me develop a clear understanding of the will of Christ and to be able to present Him to the world from an unclouded perspective. By observing their excellence in ministry I was able to develop what God had deposited within me when He ordained me before I was formed in my mother's womb.

As I mentioned earlier, God is not interested in our ability, but our availability. Our broken and wounded lives give even greater credence to His healing and restorative power, because when He elevates us from positions of hopelessness to plateaus of productivity, people will know that it was His power alone that made the change. At Grace Tabernacle Church we call this a "Nobody but Jesus Transformation."

Remember, Jesus must shine in us through His Word before we will ever be able to shine for Him to the world. We can be much more effective in ministry when we embrace, practice, and allow His Word to shine in and through our lives. Keep your guard up and never allow any other advice to contaminate His Word in your heart.

CONFIDENT GODLY DEPENDENCE

Paul concludes verse 16 by saying, "I did not immediately confer with flesh and blood." His commitment to accomplish what Jesus had called him to led to a confident godly dependence in his life.

Paul learned how to lean and depend on "nobody but Jesus." He did not rely on anyone's personal opinions or advice. He did not read a horoscope before following Jesus. He did not discuss the matter with family members. Paul emphatically says, "I did not immediately confer with flesh and blood."

We may encounter people who will never understand our aggressive approach to ministry and the hours we give of our time for God's glory. But our confidence is made firm when we understand that we are following the mandate of an unseen authority who speaks to us and reassures us.

I believe *immediately* is the operative word in this verse. It suggests no hesitation, no uncertainty, no vacillation, and no indecisiveness. God wants our allegiance to Him to be instant. His track record speaks for itself. He offers us opportunities to represent Him in this world, and He promises us eternal life in His presence in a land of glorious serendipity and splendor beyond description. When God has spoken, His voice is the only one we need to hear.

A WORD FOR PASTOR AND LEADERS

One of the most difficult challenges we face as leaders is the odious task of having a board, committee, or group to approve what we know God is leading us to accomplish. I do not believe the church is a democracy where the majority rules. If that were true, the children of Israel never would have entered the Promised Land because ten of the twelve spies said they were unable to possess it. The church does not operate under a dictatorship where one man rules by the might of his personal power. The church is a theocracy. God rules through His Word as He speaks to and through His assigned leader. Whenever God has given a leader a specific vision for ministry and we make the mistake of allowing other people to squash it and cause us to change our minds, we have just become guilty of listening to people more than God.

That said, we must not believe all our dreams, desires, and ego-pacifying ideas are visions from God. We must be careful not to pursue something just because it seems to be successful in another venue. God will reveal to you plainly and distinctly what He has for your ministry. If we obey Him, it will come to pass. We may lose some friends and followers along the way, but He will always replace them with the persons we need to bring the vision to fruition.

sit here and just read on my own and reflect on th

encounter with my teachers has made on me."

would respond by saying, "Yes, you have the

teachers, but the teachers are there to help

tion in the books and to establish pers

This principle and truth is eve

Every new believer should have

son has had a personal enco

is going to grow and de

herd (pastor) to help

The young s

contacts of s

tance of t

techn

isol

Rejoice with me, for I have found ...,
to you that likewise there will be more joy in heaven over one
sinner who repents than over ninety-nine just persons who need
no repentance.

LUKE 15:4–7

*W*henever I hear a person say, "I am saved, I know how to read my Bible, and I have no need to attend a church on a regular basis," I cringe. From my vantage point this is tantamount to a child enrolling in school on the first day of class, meeting the teachers, collecting math, science, history, and English books, and then going home. The next morning, in response to his parent's request to get up and get ready for school, the child says, "I have my books, I have met my teachers, so I think I will e impression my one

Any responsible parent

books and you have met the

you to understand the informa-

onal relationships with you."

h stronger from a spiritual perspective.

a Bible, and a conversion is proof the per-

unter with Jesus Christ. But if the new believer

elop, the person needs to be connected to a shep-

gain understanding of the Word of God.

nt also needs to be connected to other sheep to establish

pport and fellowship and to better understand the impor-

e family of God. One of the sad commentaries on our advanced

logical and computerized society is that many people have become

ated. We have, in some instances, begun to feel that we have no real need to be connected to the church of God and to the shepherd God has placed and positioned as the one who watches over our souls. (See Hebrews 13:17.)

In Luke 15 Jesus gives us a perfect pictorial panoramic presentation in what I call "3D"—three divine demonstrations—of God's love for the lost. In the first two verses we read of some of the most heartwarming and informative aspects of the personality of Jesus Christ. We are told that tax collectors and sinners were able to come near to Him and in spite of opposition from the Pharisees and scribes, He received them, ate with them, and fellowshipped with them. This may seem trivial on the surface, but none of us would be saved and forgiven today if Jesus hadn't been loving enough to receive us in spite of our sinful condition.

Luke 15 presents three lost-and-found stories. Each one illustrates a different cause for being lost but only one way to be found: through Jesus. In the first story the sheep was lost because it wandered away, taking its eyes off the shepherd. The coin was lost because the woman was not responsible with all that had been placed in her care—much like many parents today whose children who are lost through no fault of their own. But because their parents have become preoccupied with other things, the children slip right through their parental care. Then, in the third story, the son was lost because of rebellion. He wanted what he thought he deserved, and he did not want to have to work or wait for it.

In this chapter we will focus on Luke 15:4–7. Jesus begins this story by talking about a man with one hundred sheep. He poses a thought-provoking question at the beginning of verse 4: "What man of you…?" implying that all persons are not equipped to properly feed, lead, and care for the sheep of God. He also tells us the number of the sheep: one hundred. I cannot emphasize enough how vitally important this is. If the shepherd did not know the exact number of his sheep, he would have no way to determine if any of them had wandered away or how many of them were lost. This is one reason I believe it is important for sheep (members of a local church) to be connected to a shepherd (pastor) who knows them and is known by them.

This may seem somewhat unrealistic from a mega-church perspective, but I hold fast to the belief that even if a shepherd is unable to interact with each of his sheep because of the size of his congregation, there must be a system in place for them to be regularly accounted for. We may not want to acknowledge or admit to it, but many persons join larger churches with the intent of getting lost in the crowd.

This story in Luke 15 gives credibility and validity to at least two basic principles. First of all, every sheep should be missed when it is away from the fold. Secondly, every sheep is valuable to God and the shepherd. If this were not true, the shepherd would not have searched for it when it strayed.

As I mentioned in chapter 2, we have in our church "tribe" ministries. The ministry consists of twelve teams with three members on each team.

One man—a preacher, deacon, or disciple—gives leadership to the team that also includes two women. We have divided our church roll alphabetically and equally into twelve groups. The men call men and pray for and with them and encourage them at least once each week, while the women do the same for the other women in the church. They then make a weekly report to a tribe ministry coordinator, who reports to me concerning any issues, such as a death in family, upcoming surgery, a relocation, or ministry apprehensions. This helps us to keep up with all of our sheep, and it also gives every new member a person of contact and care. My administrative assistant prints a new roll for me each week after any new people join our congregation and we purge our roll every three months. If we are unable to contact any members by phone, mail, email, or personal visit, we remove them from our roll. (I will say more about this system at the end of the chapter.)

I have also taken on the personal responsibility of praying for each member of the Grace Tabernacle Church family every week. My copy of the church roll is divided into six pages, and I lift the names and special needs of those individuals in prayer each week.

This may be difficult for pastors with more than a thousand members. My suggestion to you would be to divide your roll into thirty sections and pray for thirty to thirty-five people each day.

I firmly believe that people need to be connected to a church with a shepherd who keeps them covered with prayer and that sheep have a right to expect this kind of covering.

My biblical foundation for this belief is found is Acts 6:4, where the disciples said, "But we will give ourselves continually to prayer and to the ministry of the word." Please don't miss the fact that this church had at least five thousand members and they were all new converts. (See Acts 4:4.)

I also contend that it is difficult, if not impossible, for new believers to grow, mature, and develop as children of God without being personally connected to some seasoned saints who are already a part of that body of believers. God never sends us to a congregation just to blend in; He expects us to enhance the ministry and to build up others after we have become established in our relationship with Jesus Christ.

It should bring great joy to our hearts to know God loves us and values His relationship with us so much that He comes looking for us (or sends someone to look for us) to bring us back to the fold. Real love reaches out, real love searches, and real love has no limits.

The shepherd has his responsibility, but the sheep have a task as well. As members of the body of Christ, we must be consistent in our attendance and activity so when we are absent due to illness, job changes, or other matters, we will be missed by the family within two or three weeks.

I realize work schedules may prevent some of us from attending every Sunday. For this reason we need to be connected to churches with ministries during the week—women's ministries, men's ministries, and Bible studies, just to name a few. We should devote at least one day each week to fellowshipping with the people of God and studying the Word of God. If your calendar does not allow for this, then I make no apologies for saying, "You are entirely *too busy*!

We must never lose focus on the importance of joining and participating in a local church after we are born into the family of God. When we remember who (Jesus) has birthed us into the kingdom, and the price He paid for our salvation, we should have a great desire to immediately establish relationships and learn our responsibilities both with and to our brothers and sisters in Christ.

Because the sheep strayed, the shepherd was forced to leave the other sheep to go and search for it. Very few people realize how it pains the heart of a true shepherd when someone is lured away from the fold. In addition, a straying sheep causes other matters of ministry importance to be placed on hold while the shepherd searches either literally or figuratively in prayer.

I mentioned earlier in this chapter that this sheep aimlessly wandered away because it took its eyes off the shepherd. This is one of the great deceptive tactics the devil employs on the people of God even today. We have been lulled into thinking if we are not angry, upset, or in rebellion against the shepherd, then our absence is really not that serious. However, we overlook the fact that the devil specializes in causing us to become preoccupied with things that may not appear to be sinful and ungodly on the surface, but they distract us from our commitment to the Lord and His church.

We allow jobs, relationships, possessions, and even times of personal difficulty to cause us to stray from the fold. Yet, in spite of our behavior, God loves us enough to send someone to look for us until we are found. This story helped me to understand how valuable every soul is to God. He loves us enough to save us through the death of His Son, and He also loves us enough to search for us when we stray into danger.

I see at least three advantages to being connected to a shepherd and other sheep. First, we have a faithful covering.

A FAITHFUL COVERING

God has not trusted your soul to just anyone. Jeremiah 3:15 reads, "And I will give you shepherds according to My heart, who will feed you with knowledge and understanding." This is one reason we should pray fervently before we join or leave a church. God knows we need to be fed and developed, and He will not lead us to a place that will not meet these needs.

We may not want to acknowledge the truth of it, but many people join churches for the wrong reasons. Some join because it seems to be a popular place. Others join because friends and family are there. Others join because they're bitter about the church they just left, and still others join churches because they want to be challenged or held accountable for sinful activities in their lives.

Our primary reason for becoming a part of a church family should be a result of our prayerful persistent pursuit of God's will and our obedience to His guidance. God does give us shepherds, but Jesus also taught us, "Seek and you shall find." This does not mean we seek a shepherd who pleases us, but we seek for the place God wants to position us.

Our faithful covering in a shepherd consist of some basic qualities. He is *compassionate* toward the sheep. We should be able to feel the love he has for the people God has trusted to his care. He is *challenging* to the sheep, moving us out of our comfort zones. We were created by God to mature as believers, and complacency should be completely eradicated from our vocabulary and our personal demeanor. He is one who preaches a message of *conviction*. I shudder to think what would happen to my physical health if I sought out a medical specialist who told me only what I wanted to hear. Likewise, the shepherd must point out those spiritually sick areas in our lives and then tell us how we can be healed from ungodly behavior through the grace and Word of God.

A FAMILY OF CONNECTIVITY

In Luke 15, after the shepherd found the sheep, he brought it back home to the other sheep. The shepherd provides a family of connectivity.

God created us to be sources of strength and support to each other. Many people have abandoned their relationships with shepherd and sheep because of personal difficulties, not realizing that others in their church families have faced the same struggles.

God has allowed me to experience many things that seemed to be overwhelmingly inexplicable at the time I was going through them. But I later discovered God was doing at least two things through those experiences: He was strengthening my faith, and He was preparing me to later minister to someone who would face what I had faced. My life became a testimony to the fact that God has no favorites. Since He had brought me through it, I was equipped to tell someone else that He is also able to bring them through it.

When we share with other family members in the body of Christ, we can grow just from their very presence and devotion. When we see those who have gone through severe sicknesses, divorces, bankruptcy, foreclosures, repossessions, or unemployment without losing their praise and loyalty to the Lord, we are helped during our times of rigorous struggle.

Jesus also said, "It rains on the just and the unjust." God can allow His rain to wash away the iniquity of the sinful and fertilize the crops of the righteous at the same time. I call this "God's inexplicable equity." Being connected to a shepherd and other sheep encourages me during times of difficulty, and it enlightens me in my daily devotion. We are not alone; others have experienced pain, suffering, and trials that mirror our own.

FAVORED WITH CELEBRATION

Being part of the body of Christ also favors us with celebration. This text in Luke 15 also helped me understand that God doesn't limit His love to just looking for us, searching till He finds us, and bringing us back home. He also throws a party and puts us at the center of the celebration! Jesus said the shepherd calls his friends and neighbors and tells them to come celebrate with him because his lost sheep has been found.

I truly believe one of the main reasons God allows His people to consistently gather each week in worship, study of His Word, and ministry is because He is arranging celebrations for sinners and backsliders to have an opportunity to come back to Him in a triumphant environment. Dr. Freddie Dunn of New Orleans used to say, "You cannot clean a fish before you catch the fish." God knows the discipline required to prevent the sheep from straying again, but according to this story, this is not the shepherd's initial act. Our hearts to leap for joy to know God loved us enough to give us a celebration when we were found by His grace. Then He can use us to search for others who are lost and bring them into the atmosphere of a genuine godly gala. Praise God for His majestic, immeasurable love for us that caused Him to provide the church and the shepherd who will not only find us but also bring us back to the place of His favor and His development.

A WORD FOR PASTORS AND LEADERS

I mentioned our "tribes" ministry earlier in the chapter. We have twelve tribes, but the number isn't necessarily important. Adjust the system to the size of your congregation. For example, try a seven- or four-tribe system for a smaller congregation. If your congregation is larger, you might use a twenty-four- or forty-eight-tribe system. The idea behind it all is to put in place a system that allows you to connect to all of your sheep either directly or indirectly. The challenge to the leaders and tribe members is to be faithful and consistent in their weekly calls and prayers. The calls and prayers do not need to be lengthy; rather, they should be direct and to the point. I recommend our tribe teams limit their calls to between two and three minutes. If the members are not reached directly, then prayers are left on their voice mails.

For about the last three years, I have prayed for about thirty pastors each week, yet I only speak directly with five to seven of them. Job 42:10 says, "And the Lord restored Job's losses when he prayed for his friends. Indeed the Lord gave Job twice as much as he had before." Praying for my friends has helped me during some of the darkest hours in my life and ministry.

I also mentioned that we purge our church roll every three months. This helps us to know exactly how many active members we have. In addition, we delete the names of those we have not been able to contact in a ninety-day period. (Many pastors don't like to do this because their egos will be deflated when they juxtapose the actual number of regular attenders with the number they claim to have on their roll.) If those people return to our church, we add them back to the roll. This process helps me greatly because it gives me the blessing of being able to identify with the sheep God has placed under my care.

6

The Benefits and Blessings of Backup
for Burnout in Ministry

But we, brethren, having been taken away from you for a
short time in presence, not in heart, endeavored more eagerly to see
your face with great desire. Therefore we wanted to come to you—
even I, Paul, time and again—but satan hindered us. For what is
our hope, or joy, or crown of rejoicing? Is it not even you in the
presence of our Lord Jesus Christ at His coming? For you are our
glory and joy.... Therefore, when we could no longer endure it, we
thought it good to be left in Athens alone, and sent Timothy, our
brother and minister of God, and our fellow laborer in the gospel
of Christ, to establish you and encourage you concerning your
faith, that no one should be shaken by these afflictions; for you
yourselves know that we are appointed to this. For, in fact, we told
you before when we were with you that we would suffer tribula-
tion, just as it happened, and you know. For this reason, when I
could no longer endure it, I sent to know your faith, lest by some
means the tempter had tempted you, and our labor might be in
vain.

1 THESSALONIANS 2:17–20; 3:1–5

In June of 2008 at approximately 9:15 a.m. I endured one of the most
frightening experiences of my life. I had just finished preaching in our

early worship experience, extended the invitation to Christian discipleship, and united four new people with our church family. I then walked out of the pulpit and headed down the hall to my study to change clothes and prepare to teach our new members' orientation class at 9:30 and then preach in the midmorning worship after that. On the way to my office, I felt lightheaded and began to lose my balance. By the grace of God, two of my sons in the ministry were walking with me, and as I began to almost faint, they held me up and helped me to my study. One of the nurses at our church went to her car, retrieved her equipment, and took my blood pressure, which was 188 over 124. I did not realize the severity of those numbers at the time, but those attending me did. I thought all I needed to do was relax for a few minutes and I would be ready to preach in the next worship experience. Those precious people who were with me in my study insisted that I be immediately taken to the emergency room. I acquiesced, and off we went.

After testing and examination in the ER, I was informed that I was experiencing apprehension and hypertension. In a subsequent visit to my primary physician he recommended that I take a break from the multitude of responsibilities I shouldered and allow my body to heal. I shared his recommendation with my staff and our congregation, and from that experience came the content of this chapter.

I have always attempted to base everything we do in our church on the foundation of the Word of God. But at that point I was dealing with issues I did not know how to properly process from a spiritual vantage point. I must admit that I did ask God why this was happening to me and what I had done to bring this on myself. I thought I was doing my best to accomplish His will and to lead His people with a "spirit of excellence." Yet here I was being told that I needed to slow down, regroup, and reprioritize my daily responsibilities. I initially struggled to process these events. I wanted to make sure there was a biblical paradigm to follow, or at least to use as an example for my own spiritual strengthening.

While I was resting and recovering, the Spirit of the Lord led me to 1 Thessalonians during my morning devotional reading. When I arrived at chapter 2, I read about some of Paul's difficulties in his ministry, as well as his words of encouragement to the Thessalonian church concerning their present and future hardships.

When I read verse 17 and a few of the following verses, the Lord spoke to my heart and helped me understand why I was going through my particular trial. Verses 17 and 18 really set the tone for my spiritual refreshing: "But we, brethren, having been taken away from you for a short time in presence, not in heart, endeavored more eagerly to see your face with great desire. Therefore we wanted to come to you—even I, Paul, time and again—but satan hindered us."

I realized then from the truth I had read from the Word of God that what I experienced was an attack from satan. I also knew that if God had allowed it, He had a purpose in mind for my life, my ministry, our church family, and the kingdom of God as a whole.

I discovered that it does not matter how loyal, committed, and dedicated we are to the work of God, our bodies eventually reach their limit and need to be refreshed and restored. Below is a list of some of my responsibilities that led to this life-changing experience:

- 2000: God used me to lead our church into remodeling an old building on our property and opening an outreach center called "Garments and Groceries from Grace." We used it to minister to those who were less fortunate in our community.
- 2001: As our church began to grow, we expanded our parking lot.
- 2002: We remodeled our facility and added an overflow to accommodate the new growth.

- 2003: We built a children's and youth center to meet the needs of our future generations.
- 2004: We purchased the six-plus acres of land where our present church is now located.
- 2005: We started construction on our new church campus.
- 2006: In May we were blessed by God to complete the first phase of our building project.
- 2007: In July we completed the second phase of our building project. I took responsibility for overseeing all the details of each project, and God gave me the grace to fulfill these assignments.

While all this was happening, I was also preaching three or four times on Sundays, leading ten to fifteen revivals per year, developing sons and daughters in ministry, training disciples and deacons, serving as chairman of the board of directors for a minority adoption agency called "One Church One Child," and preaching in twenty to twenty-five Annual Day invitations. I was also striving to be a good husband to my wife, a good father to my children, and a good pastor to our church.

Then, when my physical episode happened in June 2008, I realized God had not left me. He simply wanted to replenish me so He could use me at a maximum level in the future. I also realized satan attacks those who are seeking to do God's will because, from his perspective, serious harm is about to affect his influence in the lives of both saved and unsaved people.

Reading Paul's testimony in 1 Thessalonians did several things for me. First, it helped me realize I was not alone in my struggle. Second, it gave me an opportunity to learn how to properly balance the demands of ministry. Third—and this will be the primary focus of this chapter—it gave me a chance to watch those in whom I had planted so much step up to the plate and fulfill various roles during my time of healing.

My sons and daughters in ministry met and mapped out a preaching rotation that gave me thirty days of rest with very limited responsibilities, and they did it without any internal disagreements. I told them both privately and publicly how grateful I was to God for them and for how they did not allow any areas of ministry to suffer because of my temporary absence.

I hear many pastors complain about the lack of support and loyalty they receive from their associate ministers. They expect associates to attend conferences and workshops to teach them how to better serve in ministry. My experience, however, has taught me that loyalty from ministers and leaders does not come by way of conferences and workshops but by establishing genuine personal relationships with them. I have learned to treat them not like "associates" only, but as fellow brothers and sisters in ministry who have partnered with me to accomplish the work of the kingdom. I thank God that He has positioned these ministers with me as assets and not liabilities. While there have been a few exceptions, I will take some responsibility for not solidifying those relationships. I still enjoy close relationships even with those who have been placed by God to lead their own congregations. The men and women of God who have surrounded me have truly been a blessing from Him. When I was going through my serious attack from the devil, they personified what true backup in ministry is all about.

> In 1 Thessalonians 2:17, Paul expresses the eager intensity and great desire he had to see these people whom he loved dearly. This helped me to understand when the *hopes of our heart* are in the right place, God's *hand of help* will always be available, accessible, and able.

Many times people use general fatigue related to long work hours, children involved in several extracurricular activities, stress in the home, or financial difficulties as an excuse for taking a break from their ministry responsibilities. However, none of these fit the category Paul is addressing in this passage. He is referring only to the burnout he was experiencing from his God-given ministry assignments. He said in verse 18 he wanted to come time and time again, but satan hindered him and his ministry team. The real crux of this passage is found in 3:1–2. He says, "Therefore, when we could no longer endure it, we thought it good to be left in Athens alone, and sent Timothy, our brother and minister of God, and our fellow laborer in the gospel of Christ, to establish you and encourage you concerning your faith." Here Paul makes a declaration of honesty.

DECLARATION OF HONESTY

Paul is transparent enough to share with us that his heart, soul, and mind wanted to see the Thessalonians, but his body was too weak from the satanic attacks against him to make the journey. This was not an excuse; this was the reality of his condition. I mentioned earlier that many of us are unable to apply this principle because we do not suffer from burnout in ministry, we suffer from burnout from doing what we think will make our lives complete. The end result is we become too weary to offer any quality and consistent ministry either to or for the Lord.

The historical research on this passage helps us to understand that there were some Christian brothers and sisters in Athens who had advised Paul not to make this journey because they knew his physical condition. I believe it is always good to surround yourself with people who are spiritually sensitive to God's voice. They will be able to offer sound godly advice during our times of tremendous difficulty. We will never be able to help others until we can be totally honest with God and ourselves. I believe Paul spent this time in Athens being spiritually refreshed.

> The paramount principle: *Spiritual rest* should lead to
> a *spiritual return* so that we might be better able to
> accomplish our *spiritual responsibilities*.

He tells us in verse 2 of chapter 3 that he sent Timothy to them to establish and encourage them concerning their faith. After his declaration of honesty, he then speaks to us concerning his dependable help.

DEPENDABLE HELP

He sends Timothy in his place. This bit of information gives us an opportunity to make an honest self-evaluation: How many of us are prepared to fill in, as Timothy did, for the burnout our leaders may experience, as Paul did? Too many times the body of Christ suffers because we have too many of what I like to call "malfunctioning sponges." We are surrounded with people who do a good job of soaking up the gospel as it is preached and taught, but they are never available to squeeze out the gospel into the lives of others.

Paul refers to Timothy first as a brother. He was a man who was near and dear to Paul's heart. This shows us the need to establish close relationships with those we worship and work with in ministry. Evidently Timothy had watched Paul closely as he was being mentored, and Paul had set a noble example that was worthy of reproduction.

What kind of example are we setting before those who work closely with us in ministry? Is it a Sunday-only example? Is it a "Do as I say and not as I do" example? Is it a grumbling or dishonest example? We must be very careful concerning the patterns we establish, because people often copy our weaknesses before they copy our strengths.

Not only does Paul refer to Timothy as a brother, but also as a minister of God. Our loyalties must extend beyond human personalities. Whatever we do in ministry should be done for God's glory. This is why we must always be prepared to fill in for those who are being viciously or temporarily attacked by satan. The manner in which we exercise our assignments will reflect either positively or negatively on our Christ. We will either help to develop the body of Christ or, if we are ill prepared, we can do serious harm to the body. I cannot stress enough the importance of each believer viewing him- or herself as a minister of God. Many of us were reared in a culture that led us to believe a minister was one who stood behind the pulpit and preached or taught the Word of God on Sundays. But the word *minister* in its purest form literally means a "servant." Even Jesus, the only begotten Son of God, said in Matthew 20:28, "Just as the Son of Man did not come to be served, but to serve, and to give His life a ransom for many." I have often wondered why is it so difficult for us to prepare ourselves to serve one another, when this is exactly what Jesus did. He had all power and no sin, and He was eager to serve; we have no power and are polluted with sin, and we are so very hesitant to serve.

Let's compare for a moment the Sunday worship experience to filling up one's fuel tank at a gas station. We would be considered prime candidates for a mental hospital if we filled our cars with gas, then turned on the engine and sat still in the parking lot or drove around in circles there, using all the fuel. The purpose of filling up is to enable us to make progress and move from one position to another.

> **Many of us make the mistake of filling up on the Word of God through sermons and Bible study lessons, then using all our energy at the church. We never grow to a point where our effectiveness touches people beyond the four walls of the building.**

Real ministry is mobile. We must move beyond a treadmill mentality, where we work up a sweat but never make any progress. God has positioned us to be ready to fill in for those who become overwhelmed by the demands of leadership and attacks from the devil.

Consider two important questions: Do you consider yourself to be a source of dependable help for a burned-out leader? If not, what steps are you taking to prepare yourself to be used by God as an effective tool in ministry? We were not saved just to sit and shout; we were saved to surrender and serve. I know some may consider this to be a cliché, but it is appropriate in helping us to understand our primary roles and responsibilities as believers.

In verse 2 of chapter 3, Paul calls Timothy a "fellow laborer in the gospel." I do not consider myself to be a Greek scholar, but I do know the word *laborer* simply means one who is willing to engage in hard work. Notice carefully, he does not call him just a laborer, but a fellow laborer. They worked together. They had established a bond of Christian cohesiveness. They supported of each other. They went through their struggles together. And behind it all we find a spiritual purpose, which we discover at the end of verse 2: "… to establish you and encourage you concerning your faith." Paul was confident that Timothy would be able to help these new believers to remain stable in their relationship with Christ and comfort them during their times of difficulty.

We need more people to fill these roles. Even sports teams know their starting players may be injured, so they have prepared backups to fill in if the starters are hurt. They have more players on the team than what are required on the field at one time. Likewise, all the members in the body of Christ should be equipping themselves to fill in for those leaders who have been wounded doing the work of the Master.

We can see the seriousness of this matter in verse 5, where Paul says, "For this reason, when I could no longer endure it, I sent to know your faith, lest by some means the tempter had tempted you, and our labor might be in vain." After his declaration of honesty and his announcement of dependable help, he then shares words of his disposition of hopefulness.

DISPOSITION OF HOPEFULNESS

I can almost feel the pain in Paul's heart when he says "When I could no longer endure it." He wanted to get to them, but he had reached his physical limit. Yet in his soul he still had their spiritual well-being at the apex of his hopes. He wanted to know the condition of their faith, and he was able to send someone. This may seem simple on the surface, but take a moment to consider the entire equation. I cannot help but believe his progress and recovery were accelerated when Timothy went to minister to these precious people on Paul's behalf, then brought word back to him concerning their progress, stability, and faithfulness.

Knowing the ministries of the church are thriving in his absence can help a leader heal more quickly. Learning that his people have not yielded to the tempter through divisiveness brings delight to a pastor's heart. Seeing that his labor has not been in vain eases a leader's mind. Hope gives encouragement to the heart and brings healing to the mind and body.

I will conclude here by sharing with you how God has healed me, given me the grace to return to my responsibilities, and filled me with gratitude for leaders and members who stepped up and filled in during my illness. The Lord's church did not suffer any loss or lack, and it was all because people were in place to serve as backup for the burnout their leader was experiencing. I would love for your pastor to be able to say the same about you!

A WORD FOR PASTORS AND LEADERS

Quality backup in our churches and ministries will not happen automatically. We must spend time investing our energy, our resources, and ourselves into the lives of those God has positioned around us. We must give them some hands-on experience. Be patient with them when they make mistakes and show them how to make the necessary corrections.

I cannot emphasize enough the importance of establishing close personal relationships with those who have the potential of a Timothy. Everyone will not fit this category, so we must pray and be prepared before the tempter overwhelms us. If you feel your load of ministry seems more difficult that you can manage alone, ask God for help rather than randomly selecting someone you think will fill that role.

I am a witness to the fact that He always places in every church just what every church needs. You may not see it now, but I can say by faith that your church or ministry is pregnant with potential. Keep fueling them, keep feeding them, remain faithful to them, and watch God formulate them to fill those temporary voids of weariness that arise in all of our lives and ministries. Be blessed and be encouraged. God's got your back!

7

Making the Best of What You Have

For the kingdom of heaven is like a man traveling to a far country, who called his own servants and delivered his goods to them. And to one he gave five talents, to another two, and to another one, to each according to his own ability; and immediately he went on a journey. Then he who had received the five talents went and traded with them, and made another five talents. And likewise he who had received two gained two more also. But he who had received one went and dug in the ground, and hid his lord's money. After a long time the lord of those servants came and settled accounts with them. So he who had received five talents came and brought five other talents, saying, "Lord, you delivered to me five talents; look, I have gained five more talents besides them." His lord said to him, "Well done, good and faithful servant; you were faithful over a few things, I will make you ruler over many things. Enter into the joy of your lord." He also who had received two talents came and said, "Lord, you delivered to me two talents; look, I have gained two more talents besides them." His lord said to him, "Well done, good and faithful servant; you have been faithful over a few things, I will make you ruler over many things. Enter into the joy of your lord." Then he who had received the one talent came and said, "Lord, I knew you to be a hard man, reaping where you have not sown, and gathering where you have not scattered seed. And I was afraid, and went and hid your talent in the ground. Look, there you have what is yours." But his lord answered and said to him, "You wicked and lazy servant, you knew that I reap where I have not sown, and gather where I have not scattered seed. So you ought to have deposited my money with the bankers, and at my coming I would have received back my own with interest. So take the talent from him, and give it to him who has ten talents. For to everyone who has, more will be given, and he will have abundance; but from him who does not have, even what he has will be taken away."

MATTHEW 25:14–29

*I*t may seem obvious and elementary on the surface, but many churches, ministries, and ministers suffer disappointment and frustration because they fail to fully utilize what God has provided for them. We have a humanistic tendency to focus on and become obsessively preoccupied with the exterior successes that others seem to be enjoying without being grateful to God for the opportunities and assignments He has trusted us with.

I mentioned in the introduction that one of my good friends, Dr. Ralph West, said to me many years ago when we were both struggling to build young churches, "God places some fish in ponds and others in oceans." I have now added to that statement, "All the fish belong to God." He knows what we can handle, and He knows where our ministries will be most effective.

Many pastors and leaders don't consider that all people are not comfortable in mega-churches. Some are interested in smaller congregations where they will have an opportunity to interact regularly with people they have come to know. This is not to suggest churches should not seek new growth and pursue the God-given assignment of making disciples, but I say unapologetically that congregants in smaller churches also deserve quality, compassion. and vision from their leadership.

> We must stop thinking we'll be comfortable and complacent where we are until something larger, better, or more lucrative (in our estimation) comes along.

God knows the qualities He has deposited within each of us, and He expects us to use what He's given us to His glory. Those of us who are engaged or married would be seriously offended and emotionally wounded if we discovered our mate intended to be part of our lives only until someone better came along. Ministry leadership and even ministry participation are serious responsibilities God has given to us. We should not approach either one of them lightly, with a flippant or lackadaisical attitude.

> We see the exterior successes of others, but we seldom see the internal strain, struggle, and sacrifice God required them to make to achieve that success.

Many things related to my ministry bring a tremendous amount of joy to my heart. But I'm overwhelmed when I consider that what God has trusted me with is far more than I deserve. In our society, even among believers, we cultivate an attitude of entitlement. We feel as though God owes us something, and we have a right to expect nothing but pleasure, peace, and prosperity from Him. In truth, it is an honor and a privilege to have been saved by God through His Son Jesus Christ and filled with His precious Holy Spirit. This may seem too familiar or even insignificant on the surface, but when we stop to consider the wretched condition of our hearts and souls before we met the Lord, very few of us would allow our spirits to constantly abide in such environments. We have ungodly thoughts, we commit ungodly acts, we say ungodly things, and we behave in ungodly ways. I believe Isaiah described it best when he said in chapter 6 verse 5 of his prophecy, "Woe is me, for I am undone! Because I am a man of unclean lips, and I dwell in the midst of people of unclean lips." Yet through God's forgiveness, mercy, and grace, He still chooses to live in us and desires to work through us.

Readjust your mind-set for a moment from considering ministry as a laborious chore to embracing it as a delightful privilege from God. When we make this shift, we can maximize our potential right where we have been perfectly and purposefully planted and positioned by God. God wants to use each of us to make a positive difference in the lives of those we touch and those whom He sends across our paths.

If we are going to be successful in this venture, we must incorporate at least three primary elements into our hearts and minds.

1. AN AWARENESS OF GOD'S PRESENCE

We are not where we are by accident; we have been perfectly positioned by divine providence. We may not have all we think we deserve, we may be going through pain we cannot explain, or we may be faced with demonic dissuasions when we have tried our very best to do our very best. But yet, we must firmly believe we are not in this alone. God is with us! When inexplicable circumstances arise in my life, I gain the strength to go on and press my way through when I remember that as long as God is keeping me alive, He still has some positive and productive work left for me to accomplish. We must take our eyes off of the struggle and focus more on the power of the God who will help us to deal with the struggles.

When we know God is with us, the journey becomes worth the effort. We cannot see Him, at times we may not feel Him, and there will even be periods when He will seem to be silent to our cries of desperation. Yet, we must rest on the promise He made in His inerrant and unalterable Word in Hebrews 13:5 "I will never leave you nor forsake you." God's presence in our lives is not predicated on our behavior but on our belief in Him.

> **God wants us to be assured of His presence because it leads us to a plateau where we see life and ministry from His vast perspective and not from our limited viewpoint.**

When we are assured of God's presence in our lives and in our ministries, it will comfort us. And when I use the word *comfort* I am not suggesting complacency or a disposition of apathy. The comfort I am speaking of comes by way of

His *eternal word for our everyday situations,*
His *enabling Spirit for our enormous struggles* and
His *empowering strength for our elevating successes.*

His presence also assures us of God's compassion in our lives. Temporary failure causes us to feel defeated, hopeless, and helpless. But His presence reminds us that He does not love us because of our victories but in spite of our defeats. When our lives are totally surrendered to God, He can transform our defeats into development and our discouragements into determination.

We are valuable to God—so valuable that He allowed His Son to pay the price for our sins. We must also realize He has saved us by His grace to use us to His glory. Jesus knows the struggles we feel, He knows the temptations we face. He was even tempted at all points just like we are and yet

He was without sin. We will never face anything that is foreign or unfamiliar to Jesus Christ.

Our God is a loving, faithful, and forgiving Father. He is sacrificial in His nature, kind in His character, and patient in His disposition. We have failed to keep the promises we have made to Him, but He has never recalled, revoked, or removed our salvation. These truths should serve as models of motivation for us to make ourselves and our gifts even more available to God.

2. AN ASSURANCE OF GOD'S POWER

His presence assures us of God's challenges for our lives. But His power assures us of the ability to meet and conquer those challenges. We have a great God living within us. We are not dependent on our own power and resources but on His unlimited supremacy and His ability to use us beyond our greatest expectations. We must not allow ourselves to become relegated to redundancy when we have the potential to represent righteous royalty.

One of the statements I love to make at the Grace Tabernacle Church and everywhere I go to preach or teach is this: "Wherever you are at this point in your ministry or in your relationship with Christ, you are in a 'no parking zone.'" This is a warning against complacency. Don't ever turn your spiritual engine off! We must always be ready to move at God's command and accept God's new responsibilities for our lives—even though they may seem impossible. Challenges produce growth and determination, and they add to our testimonial résumés. Christianity and being stationary are diametrically opposed, and they have no place in the same sentence or the same conversation. We will face challenges, but they come so God's power and not ours can be seen. My mother always said, "When things are too hard for us, they are just right for God." She also loved to say, "The good Lord never places any more on us than we are able to bear."

No NFL, NBA, or Major League ballplayer is ever surprised when the opposition tries to defeat, stop, hinder or even injure him. They practice knowing they are in for a fight on game day. We as Christians must recognize that we too are in a daily battle. Paul said in Ephesians 6:12, "For we do not wrestle against flesh and blood, but against principalities, against powers, against the rulers of the darkness of this age, against spiritual hosts of wickedness in the heavenly places." I wish I had better news for you, but the truth is, living for Jesus Christ is a constant battle against the devil. The good news comes in knowing we are on the victorious side. I read the end of the book called the Bible—and we win!

Don't be surprised, then, when attacks come your way as you move higher in ministry responsibility and accountability. This is only God's way of equipping us for greater service in His kingdom.

3. An Allegiance to God's Purpose

Having an allegiance to God's purpose entails surrendering to His will and being confident that His plan for our lives will be fulfilled. This occurs as we learn to hear His voice as it is spoken through His Word. When Jesus was facing one of the darkest hours in His life in the Garden of Gethsemane, He asked His Father to remove the cup of bitterness and sin from Him, and then He surrendered with memorable words: "Not My will, but Yours, be done" (Luke 22:42). We must approach ministry by making ourselves available to complete those assignments God places before us.

A person may ask, "Why should we strive to make the best of what we have?" and "Why do we have a need to focus exclusively on what God has placed in our hands to work with"? I believe we can find the answers in Matthew 25:14–29.

The story begins with a man preparing to travel to a far country. He calls his servants to him and gives one of them five talents, another two, and to another one. Verse 15 ends with "to each according to his own ability; and immediately he went on a journey."

The three servants received something they had not worked for and that did not belong to them. One of the best ways to fully utilize our gifts from God is to first recognize we have not earned them and we certainly do not deserve them. They are gifts from Him.

GOD HAS TRUSTED US WITH HIS RESOURCES

We must remember that God has called us to Him through the process of *salvation*, He has made us fit for service through the process of *sanctification*, and now He trusts us with His possessions through the process of *stewardship*.

The word *talent* in this passage refers to money. The money did not belong to the servants, but it was placed in their trust. Every Christian must realize that we own absolutely nothing; God has entrusted to our care all we have. When we learn to handle our finances in a godly manner, we will also handle all the other aspects of our lives in a godly manner. Wherever you are serving in ministry right now, you need to know that God has trusted you with His resources.

> **Our very lives are gifts from God. In spite of our struggles, difficulties, and heartaches we have been selected by God to handle His resources. Our self-esteem should be instantly elevated just to know that the King of Kings, the Lord of Lords, the Creator of this vast universe loved us enough to place His possessions in our care.**

I have also discovered that the way we treat the gift is a reflection of how we feel about the giver. We must direct our attention away from what we don't have and learn to be grateful to God for what He has given to us.

I remember watching a television show many years ago in which the husband had purchased an expensive gift for his wife. When he presented it to her and she opened it, her first words were "Oh you shouldn't have. I don't deserve it, but I thank you for loving me enough to make the sacrifice to give this to me." When was the last time you took inventory of the many blessings God has given to you and said to Him, "Lord, You shouldn't have, but I thank You for loving me enough to make the sacrifice of giving Your Son to me and making me an eternal part of Your kingdom"?

If we are going to learn the importance of making the best of what we have, we must begin by recognizing that we have been entrusted with what we do not deserve. No matter how large or small your gift may seem to you, focus on the greatness of the Giver.

GOD HAS GIVEN US HIS RECOGNITION

The owner gave to each servant according to his own ability. God knows how much we can handle. Many people have experienced terrible plights and downfalls in life because they have been trusted with too much too fast. We have a microwave mentality; we want it all right now. But God not only knows how many burdens we can bear, He also knows how many blessings we can handle. The owner did not give every servant an equal number of talents. Perhaps he based his determination based on their past performances and faithfulness.

We must rid ourselves of the idea that God's love for us is predicated upon God's gifts to us. Many teach and believe that the more stuff we have, the more of God's favor we have. But nothing could be further from the truth. For example, I love each of my four children equally, but I do not bless each of them equally. Some blessings my older daughters can handle more responsibly than my young son could, and he has no right to question my love for him simply because I do not give to him at the same level as his sisters. As their father, I know what they are able to handle and I expect them to make the best of what I have given them. In addition, I expect them to avoid comparing themselves to one another in the process. Just like a good father, God knows our level of accountability.

> You may not be the ministry leader, but are you a good ministry follower? You may not be a pastor, but are you a source of consistent support to your pastor? You may not be the lead singer, but are you the best soprano, alto, tenor, or bass you can be?

God blesses us according to His recognition of us. He knows that too much too soon may do us more harm than good. This is part of God's developmental process. He wants to be able to trust us without our feeling threatened by His presence. I believe this is the reason the story mentions that the owner left immediately and went on a journey. God does not want us to feel hounded by Him; He wants us to feel reassured and confident by His constant abiding presence.

GOD HAS GIVEN US RESPONSIBILITIES

In the parable of the talents, one striking element is obviously missing: The owner does not tell the servants what to do with the talents; he just gives them the money and leaves. I believe the lesson we must learn from this noticeable omission is "A person with a grateful heart will always seek to expand and develop what he or she has been given to work with without needing to be told." The man with five talents invested what he had and doubled his resources. The man with two did the same. If you are despondent about not having more from God, how are you investing what you have been given? It seems to me that these two men believed their master deserved to receive not only what he had given them, but even more because of the trust and confidence he had placed in them. Often I ask the members of our congregation, "How is the kingdom of God better because God chose to make you a part of it?" Are we only occupying space, or are we investing the treasures and gifts God has given to us in the lives of those around us?

> The day of accountability is coming.

GOD WILL GIVE US REWARDS

After a long time the owner returned to settle his accounts. The man who had five talents brought him ten, and the man with two talents brought him four. He said to both of them, "Well done, good and faithful servant; you were faithful over a few things, I will make you ruler over many things." But the man who had only one talent had buried it. I cannot help but wonder, "How much buried treasure is being wasted, buried in the members of the church of Jesus Christ?"

This man's actions greatly displeased the owner, and he called the man a lazy servant. The talent he had was taken from him and given to the man who had ten. Please don't miss this! The talents had been entrusted to these men as stewards before the owner left town. Because the man with ten talents wisely invested them, he was allowed to keep all ten and was given the one from the slothful and irresponsible steward. This just may be God's way of telling us the best way to receive more from Him is to fully utilize to His glory what He has already given us.

Now, the ten-talent man had the opportunity to increase his possession to twenty-two talents. This is why the story closes with verses 29–30: "For to everyone who has, more will be given, and he will have abundance; but from him who does not have, even what he has will be taken away. And cast the unprofitable servant into outer darkness. There will be weeping and gnashing of teeth." This is a strong warning to wisely use what we have and to be grateful for the resources God has entrusted to our care.

A WORD FOR PASTORS AND LEADERS

We must always treasure our ministries. They may not be the largest in the city, but they can develop into all God would have them to be when we use to His glory, and not to our selfish aggrandizement, our time, talent, and treasure.

Don't make the mistake of measuring your success or failure by what may be going on around you. God wants to use you to develop your 50-, 75-, 125-, or 250-member congregation. Be thankful to Him for what you have, make the best of it, and watch Him multiply in His own way and in His own time.

Focus more on ministry quality and less on ministry quantity. The quality will produce growth, but when the focus is on numbers only, churches and ministries have a tendency to swell. And whenever something swells, it gets larger but it may also be infected. Growth comes through time, effort, and sacrifice. When these factors are our main focus, God will give the increase.

8

Don't Be Distracted by the Stone

Now when the Sabbath was past, Mary Magdalene, Mary the mother of James, and Salome bought spices, that they might come and anoint Him. Very early in the morning, on the first day of the week, they came to the tomb when the sun had risen. And they said among themselves, "Who will roll away the stone from the door of the tomb for us?" But when they looked up, they saw that the stone had been rolled away—for it was very large.

MARK 16:1–4

For nearly three and a half years, Jesus Christ, the immaculate Son of God, had been headed toward Calvary. All of the sermons, teachings, healings, and miracles pointed toward a date with destiny on a hill called Golgotha. His death would be much more dramatic and attention grabbing than His birth.

He arrived in obscurity and in humble surroundings. No pomp and circumstance. No marching bands. No large crowds assembled to greet the newborn King. But at His death, soldiers stood by and onlookers watched Him suffer as no man had ever suffered before. In addition, two arch enemies, Herod and Pilate, laid their differences aside in an attempt to hush the mouth of this preacher whose message could not be debated and whose miracles could not be denied.

On that Friday morning when the master, miraculous, maker of matchless mercy began His march up the Via Dolorosa, He knew He would soon experience excruciating pain, dehumanizing insults, and worst of all, the incomprehensible silence of His Father in heaven, as He cried out, "My God, My God, why have you forsaken Me?"

Finally, at the ninth hour (about three o'clock in the afternoon), Jesus cried out with a loud voice, breathed His last breath with the lungs of a man, and died.

He was not murdered, assassinated, or ambushed. Instead, He surrendered His life. Prior to His death He declared, "No one takes [My life] from Me, but I lay it down of Myself. I have power to lay it down, and I have power to take it again" (John 10:18). After He died, Nicodemus—a ruler of the Jews—and Joseph, from a town called Arimathea and a member of the Sanhedrin, went to Pilate and requested to bury the body of Jesus.

Note that Nicodemus was not the only convert from the Sanhedrin who believed in the authenticity of the ministry of Jesus. According to Mark 15:43, this other member, Joseph, who was perhaps won to Christ by Nicodemus, was also waiting for the kingdom of God. These two men went against the religious rulers of their day and risked their lives by asking for the body of Jesus. Jesus was crucified as a criminal, and under Roman law criminals were not given the right to a decent burial. But Joseph gave Jesus the tomb he had purchased for his own use. I am sure he believed Jesus when He said, "Destroy this Temple, and in three days I will raise it up." Mary and the other disciples had given Jesus a permanent burial place in their hearts, thinking they would never see Him alive again. But Joseph gave Jesus a temporary resting place in his personal tomb because he believed Jesus only needed to use it for one weekend and would return it in its previous condition.

All four Gospel writers—Matthew, Mark, Luke, and John—tell us Joseph wrapped the body of Jesus in linen cloth and laid Him in the tomb. Mark 15:46 tells us Joseph also rolled the large stone in front of the opening of the tomb. Matthew tells us that the chief priest and the Pharisees sealed the tomb and set a guard of at least twelve soldiers.

Let's examine the evidence before us. We have a dead Jesus in Joseph's tomb. The tomb has been sealed and guards have been posted in front of the large rock to make sure Jesus' disciples do not steal His body and then claim He rose from the dead.

When Mary and the other women arrive at the tomb very early Sunday morning, they have one major concern: Who will roll away the stone for us? According to Mark 15:47, Mary Magdalene and Mary the mother of Joses saw Joseph bury Jesus. They saw where He was buried and they saw the stone placed in front of the tomb.

When we arrive at Mark 16, there are three women: Mary Magdalene, Mary the mother of James, and Salome. They have with them spices and ointment, but their main problem is they are looking for a dead Jesus, whom they don't think they will get to see because of the stone.

I believe their actions and mental predisposition reveal some of the same issues we face in dealing with the stones that seem to stand between us and our Savior. Let's look at the information provided in the Word of God.

According to Matthew 27:60; Mark 15:46; and Luke 23:53, only one man, Joseph of Arimathea, rolled the stone in front of the tomb. I contend that if one man could roll a stone in front of a tomb, then surely if they were determined enough, three to eight women could have rolled a stone away from the tomb. These women were on their way to see Jesus with doubts in their hearts. They weren't sure if they would even be able to get to Him, because of some manmade barrier.

Perhaps, like those women, you doubt your ability to reach out and touch Jesus because of some barrier you saw someone place between you and your Lord. In your mind, that stone—that hurt, that pain, that memory—seems too large for you to move. But the Lord wants you to know He is able to move any obstacle anyone may place in your path.

When we consider that John says Mary the mother of Jesus was there, and Luke mentions that Joanna and other women were also there, this looks almost like a small women's ministry assembly. I could understand them asking their question if they had come to the tomb alone, but the text clearly says in verse 3, "Who will roll the stone away for *us*."

God does not want us to underestimate our collective ability. There are some issues in our lives that we cannot conquer alone. This is why every person needs to be connected to a church and ministry. Just as one man put that stone there, all it took was our God to move it out of the way. Tradition tells us this stone may have weighed as much as two thousand pounds. But that cannot be an accurate assessment because Joseph and Nicodemus together could not have moved a two-thousand-pound stone. I believe this stone was placed there to represent some barriers we may have established in our minds and hearts, but God already knows how He plans to move them. No matter what may have happened in your past, that stone cannot keep you from getting to Jesus. Maybe you were hurt by a preacher, disappointed by a deacon, mistreated by a ministry leader, or just forsaken by a congregation. God wants you to know if a person placed a stone in front of you, He has given you the power to move it, go around it, or wait on Him to dissolve it.

God's Word gives us many assurances of this principle:

- "No weapon formed against you shall prosper" (Isaiah 54:17).
- "He who is in you is greater than he who is in the world" (1 John 4:4).
- "I can do all things through Christ who strengthens me" (Philippians 4:13).
- "The Lord is my light and my salvation; whom shall I fear?" (Psalm 27:1).
- "Yea, though I walk through the valley of the shadow of death, I will fear no evil" (Psalm 23:4).

There is no stone too large, no problem too difficult, no hurt too painful, and no betrayal too severe. In other words, "Ain't no mountain high enough," no valley low enough, no river wide enough, no cost too expensive, no journey long enough, and no night dark enough to keep us from getting to Jesus. So before you question your inability to move your stones, ask yourself, Who put them there in the first place? If a person put it there, God will give us the insight to properly evaluate it, if we just learn the importance of walking by faith and working together as a team.

> Some of us are worrying about moving stones when the blessing we need is in a totally different place.
> The Jesus they were looking for was not behind that stone.

As we continue to apply this story, we are blessed through the Word of God to make another important discovery. When these women asked each other, "Who will roll the stone away for us?" they not only underestimated their collective ability by searching for Jesus in the wrong location, they also overestimated the power of the adversary of Jesus. They gave Pilate, Herod, and the soldiers more credit than they deserved. They believed the soldiers, Pilate, and Herod had more power to hold Jesus down than God had to release Jesus.

I could have understood their asking this question on Friday night or Saturday morning or afternoon. I could have even understood their actions and concerns on Saturday night. But not on Sunday morning. He had promised to rise from the grave on the third day, and yet they believed more in what they saw than in what He had said. This was a question they never needed to ask, because they had no business going to the tomb in the first place. My own experiences have taught me that life will always be filled with disappointment and heartache whenever we start looking for Jesus in places He never said He would be. If we are not careful, we will live beneath our potential because we have listened to our adversaries words about what we cannot do, and we have totally ignored what God has said we can do.

The women went to the grave planning to conduct a burial ceremony, when they should have been in Galilee preparing to lead the worship and praise for Jesus' resurrection celebration! They had spices in their hands, and ointment in their bags, when they should have had tambourines in their hands and harps in their bags.

I wish I could have rewritten just one verse in the Bible; I could have saved these women a lot of heartache. If not a whole verse, then I wish I could change just one letter and capitalize another. Mark 16:2 says, "Very early in the morning, on the first day of the week, they came to the tomb when the *sun* had risen." I would love to be able to capitalize that "s" in *sun* and change that "u" to an "o." And if I were allowed to completely rewrite the verse, it would read like this: "Very early in the morning the women woke up shouting and dancing. There was no need to even go to the tomb because they believed the *son* had *already risen!*"

But, like many of us, they heard what Jesus said, but they did not believe He had the power to keep His word. Have you made the mistake of underestimating the ability of God to work through you? Do you have an "I can't" mentality? An "I'll never get over this" mindset? A "You hurt me too bad" disposition or a "This stone is too heavy to move" attitude? Or, have you overestimated your adversary? You may be worrying about some things today that God has already rolled away. Even though these women saw Joseph place the stone there on Friday, and the soldiers sealed it on Saturday, God rolled it away early Sunday morning.

Notice one other thing about the adversary. A group of Roman soldiers were given the responsibility of standing guard outside the grave and in front of the stone. But when God raised Jesus, not even one of these men knew what had happened until later on that day. This helped me to understand that God has the power to deliver us—without even disturbing our enemy. God does not always have to kill or cripple our enemies. Sometimes He will leave our enemies right in place so they can testify that while they were trying to hold us down, God brought us out—and they won't even know how. All they know is that we have been delivered!

The women finally arrived at the tomb, "But when they looked up, they saw that the stone had been rolled away, for it was very large" (Mark 16:4). At that point they got a firsthand observation of the power of our almighty God. They went to the tomb wondering who was going to roll away the stone. They went to the tomb to pay their last respects and get out one last cry. Carefully consider these final three things that happened to the women on that first Easter Sunday morning:

1. *God redirected their focus.* The text says, "But when they looked up." Perhaps they had been looking at the ground as they walked, or maybe they were focused on the sadness and emptiness around them. Maybe all they saw was the pain in each other's faces and how the dirt was turning to mud as their tears fell to the ground. But when they decided to look up, they discovered that things were not as bad as they had supposed them to be. When they looked up, they discovered that all their worry had been in vain. The Lord allowed them to redirect their focus.

2. *The Lord removed their fear.* The text says, "They saw that the stone had been rolled away." The stone was not gone, it was just moved! And it wasn't moved to allow Jesus to get out. No, the stone was moved so we could look in and see that He was no longer in the grave. God does not always evaporate our stones. Sometimes He just changes their location.

3. *The Lord wanted them to release their faith.* Finally, the verse ends by saying the stone "was very large." After the women looked into

the tomb and saw that Jesus was no longer there, the angel told them to go tell Jesus' disciples and Peter to meet Him in Galilee. No matter how large your stone may seem to be, God can roll it away. Then, after He gets our attention He gives us an assignment. During some of the most complex seasons in our lives, God is still able to use us to accomplish His will and spread His Word. Take your eyes off that stone and focus on the Savior!

A Word for Pastors and Leaders

As leaders we all have some stones that seem to hinder us from realizing our dreams and visualizing our heartfelt desires. We must take a moment to ask ourselves, "Am I seeking God in the place where He promised He would be, or am I seeking Him just where I think and suppose Him to be?" The devil often uses people to place things in our path of progress because it is his job to attempt to stop us from doing what he knows God has called and commissioned us to do. We may have to deal with stones of leadership conflicts, financial shortages, emotional disappointments, family misunderstandings, and even internal betrayal. The life of Jesus teaches us that God uses all these things in an inexplicable way to accomplish His perfect will for our lives. Don't allow your stones of slowed growth, uncommitted leaders, lack of spiritual enthusiasm or unfulfilled expectations to cause you to abandon the purpose that God has for your life. Press on!

When my stones seemed greater than I was able to handle (I still deal with some on a daily basis), I was driven back to the promises God made in His Word. I would much rather spend my time searching His Word for answers to my difficulties than I would trying to move a stone, only to discover Jesus is no longer there.

The enemy wants you to assume Jesus is behind the stone in the graveyard because he knows you are traveling in the wrong direction and your only intent is to weep over Him. But His word says, "Meet Me in Galilee." There we will not need to weep over a dead Jesus, but we can rejoice with Him who is alive and has all power in His hands. Return to your ministry and your church determined to be used by God in greater ways than you have ever been used by Him before.

9

Reaching Beyond Our Comfort Zones

But you shall receive power when the Holy Spirit has come upon you; and you shall be witnesses to Me in Jerusalem, and in all Judea and Samaria, and to the end of the earth.

ACTS 1:8

M any years ago as a young pastor I heard Dr. Robert H. Wilson, who served then as pastor of Cornerstone Baptist Church of Christ of Dallas, Texas, make a statement that really helped open my eyes: "The Lord Jesus Christ never gave us the command to build churches and then wait for sinners to come and fill them." This helped me tremendously in my determination to transition my mind and ministry from a posture of stagnant traditionalism to a biblical model of effectively reaching out to those who do not know Christ and making disciples of those who are babes in Christ. If we are not careful, we can easily get stuck maintaining the normal routines of church attendance and activities we have passed down from one generation to another. Many of us need to admit we have worshipped or participated in church having no idea why. We simply saw people before us do it and we assumed we should follow suit.

A young girl observed her mother preparing Christmas dinner. The mother took out a ham and cut it in half and placed one half in one pan and the other half in another pan. The young girl asked her mother why she did this. The mother's response was, "Because that is how my mother did it." She went into the living room and asked her grandmother why she prepared the ham that way. Her response was, "Because that is how my mother did it." The young girl was determined to get to the bottom of the matter, so she went into her great-grandmother's bedroom and asked her about this tradition. Her response was, "I don't know why your mother and your grandmother prepare their hams like that, but I did it because I had a very large ham and small pans."

Often we do and say things as believers in Christ simply because we saw someone else do it or heard someone else say it. We fail to realize the importance of searching the Scriptures to discover the paradigm and the divine design God expects us to follow as we represent Him in the world. In Matthew 5:13, Jesus said, "You are the salt of the earth." Whenever salt touches something, the flavor changes. If you put too much salt on meat, it will taste salty. Put too much salt on corn, it will taste salty. Put too much salt on beans, they will taste salty. No one ever says this salt taste meaty, this salt taste like corn, or this salt taste like beans. The salt always stands out as the prevailing dynamic. So, too, we should be the dominant factor in our society.

Yet, if we are the salt, I cannot help but wonder why the church is beginning to look, dress, and act so much like the world, rather than the world being flavored by the power of Christ through us. We seem to have lowered our standards so that we are being changed by the world instead of changing the world.

A good place for us to begin our search for the solution is Acts 1:8. Many of us have become comfortable in our little "boxes of safety," and we overlook the mandates the Master has given us. This verse helps us to realize we have not only been made salt by Jesus, but we have also been given power by Jesus. I am no scholar, but I do know salt and power cannot be effective unless they make contact. We are God's ambassadors here on earth; we are His agents of seasoning and His instruments of enablement.

But if we have not discovered all He has made available to us, then we have no idea of the wonderful life-changing potential within us.

Acts 1:8 is the final promise Jesus made to His disciples prior to His ascension back to the right hand of His Father. When He uttered these words, they had to wait for the promise to be fulfilled. But the time of waiting is over, because His words became a reality in Acts 2. The power and presence of the Holy Spirit now lives within every believer, and He gives us the authority and the ability to carry out each assignment Jesus left for us. I have mentioned it before but it bears repeating: The devil loves nothing more than stopping or limiting the power and potential God has placed in every believer.

Many have made the mistake of assuming our problems become less and our difficulties are obliterated when we establish a soul-saving relationship with Jesus Christ. Nothing could be further from the truth. Jesus said in John 16:33, "These things I have spoken to you, that in Me you may have peace. In the world you will have tribulation; but be of good cheer, I have overcome the world."

> **The Christian life is not a life free from trouble, but we do not have to handle our trouble alone.**

God has given us spiritual armor to wear. Paul describes it as a helmet of salvation, a breastplate of righteousness, feet covered with the preparation of the gospel of peace, a shield of faith, a belt of truth, and the sword of the Spirit, which is the Word of God. The Lord would never have given us all of this equipment and protection if He planned to immunize us from the attacks of the devil.

This is perhaps another reason why many believers fail to live up to God's calling on their lives. They feel as though if they become too involved in the work of Christ, the attacks from the enemy may intensify and become more than they can handle. In truth, the attacks *will* be more than we can handle, but they will never be more than God can handle!

We must never forget that we are dependent on and defended by His power. And we can only rely on it as we do His work and obey His commands.

Jesus said to His disciples in Acts 1:8, "But you shall receive power when the Holy Spirit has come upon you." Now, however, we have received power because the Holy Spirit continuously lives within us.

It would be totally asinine to purchase a $50,000 automobile, park it in your garage, and never drive it. It would be totally illogical to purchase a $500,000 home, never spend one day living in it, and allow it to remain unused and unoccupied. It would be unreasonable to purchase a $1,000 suit, leave it to hang in the closet, and never wear it. With these examples in mind, we must ask ourselves, How much sense does it make for us to respond to Jesus' death and resurrection by just sitting in church and occupying a pew for an hour and a half every Sunday?

If we are going to properly understand and utilize the power Jesus makes available to us here in Acts 1:8, we must juxtapose this verse with what He said in Matthew 28:18–20. There He tells us what we must do, and here in Acts He tells us how to successfully complete our assignment. He does not leave us to garner our own plans or methodologies; He gives us direct instructions and reinforces us with unfailing power. There is nothing vague or ambiguous about our purpose in being a part of His kingdom or in the power that supports us to carry out His will. We are saved to serve, and the plan is right before our eyes.

> If we are going to reach beyond our comfort zone we must embrace the truth that *ministry* and *mobility* are twins.

Jesus was always on the move, and He was always looking for people who were hurting and had spiritual voids in their lives that needed to be filled. People came to Him because they knew He honored genuine faith, they had a passionate desire to be touched by Him, and they identified with Him.

When we step back from Acts 1:8 to verses 6 and 7, we see an issue that caused the disciples to become distracted. (Even today it continues to preoccupy many contemporary believers.) The disciples wanted to know if Jesus was going to restore political power back to the Israelites. They wanted to enjoy a period much like that during the reigns of kings David and Solomon. They also wanted to be free from the tyranny imposed on them by the Roman government. They wanted external and political power. They were focusing on freedom from a governmental system. Perhaps they were focusing on the opportunity to get even with the Romans because of all the havoc and oppression they had suffered. But Jesus was about to give them authority over more than a political system. He was about to equip them to handle demonic and satanic oppression.

Jesus replied, "It is not for you to know times or seasons which the Father has put in His own authority." I believe this was the Master's way of informing them that their focus was aimed in the wrong direction.

To harness their attention and move it in the right direction He said, "But you shall receive power when the Holy Spirit has come upon you; and you shall be witnesses to Me in Jerusalem, and in all Judea and Samaria, and to the end of the earth."

The first comfort zone we must address is that of our immediate environment.

COMFORT ZONE 1: IMMEDIATE ENVIRONMENT

Notice how and where Jesus says the impact of the Holy Spirit's presence in their lives would be seen first. The *how* of the matter is their ability to be witnesses of Him. This includes the power to testify about Him, and to lead other people to Him. The *where* of the matter is in Jerusalem. This represented the area they were most familiar with and the region where they spent the greatest amount of time. Many of us completely overlook the responsibility we have to be witnesses where we spend the majority of our time.

I will never forget the Saturday before the fourth Sunday in April, 1987. About twenty people were assembled in the fellowship hall of The Mount Gilead Baptist Church in Fort Worth. We were in a planning meeting to organize what was about to become the Grace Tabernacle Missionary Baptist Church. Pastor Cedric Britt had invited Pastor E. V. Hill from Los Angeles to encourage us in the faith venture we were about to undertake. He made one statement I will always remember: "This church will grow and become all God will have her to be if she never loses sight of one major fact. That fact is that there is no sinner shortage. If you will always make sinners your target audience for the message about Jesus Christ, this church will grow." His words reminded us that many of us had unsaved persons in the Jerusalem of our immediate families, our places of employment, and in our social gatherings. We had the message about Jesus Christ, but it was not until we began to use His power that we were able to watch God add to the body daily those who were being saved.

We have a tendency to take our immediate environment for granted for at least two reasons. First, we become complacent in our responsibility to witness for Christ at all times and in all places. We feel as though our task is complete when we have shared Christ with someone on just one occasion. We fail to realize the importance of repetition and the command given to us by the Lord Jesus to compel people to come to Him. Many of us have family members in our homes who do not know Jesus as their Savior. We have unsaved relatives whom we see regularly at family gatherings, yet we fail to tell them about Christ because the devil has deceived us into believing that since we are saved, they should get saved the best way they can. But nothing could be further from the truth.

Second, many of us lead double lives. One side of our personality comes forth in the company of the saints at Christian functions or in the house of the Lord. We put on our pompous and pious projection of pretense. Then the other side of our personality is revealed when we are in the midst of worldly people. We act and speak just like them, which makes it plainly impossible to witness about the life-changing power of Jesus Christ. So we choose blending in with the crowd instead of standing out above the crowd. We would rather witness where people do not know us personally. We mistakenly believe we can then keep up our façade without being forced to live in a Christlike manner at all times.

If we are going to reach beyond our comfort zones as witnesses, we must start in the area where many of us have become most comfortable—our immediate environment. Take a moment to think about the people you see on a regular basis, who are living without Christ—people with whom you have never shared the gospel. The Holy Spirit will give you power and holy boldness to speak for Him. Then you will experience great joy when you see Him change their lives in the same way He has changed yours. But it all begins with our witness and His power.

COMFORT ZONE 2: EXTENDED ENVIRONMENT

Jesus does not limit the scope of the disciples' witnessing assignment to Jerusalem. Next He moves them to "Judea." I believe Judea represents those areas and people we come into contact with on an occasional basis. I also believe God allows everything to happen for a specific purpose. Sometimes God allows people to cross our paths unexpectedly, and His purpose could very well be to give them an opportunity to hear about His unconditional love from an unanticipated source. These encounters also provide us with an opportunity to be prepared to share our testimony.

One of the tremendous things about being a witness for Christ comes by way of the definition of the word. A witness is one who is required to tell only what he or she has seen and experienced. Whatever Jesus has done for us is all He expects us to share with others. We don't have to rehearse our story, we don't have to write it down, and we have no need to add to it or take away from it. We just need to share it every time we have a chance.

I am working on this chapter in January 2009. I plan to challenge each active member in our congregation to win at least one person to Christ this year. We have nearly five hundred people on our church roll—including adults, youth, and children—which means if every person brought just one person to Christ, our membership could double in one year. In Acts 2 after the Holy Spirit had manifested His presence on the Day of Pentecost, the Lord used 120 believers to win and baptize 3,000 new converts to Christianity. He did it then and He is able to do it through us even today!

> **Jesus never would have told us to witness in Jerusalem and Judea unless He knew there would be people who needed to hear about Him and people who would be won to Him.**

Jesus' command to witness is also filled with potential for spiritual success. He directs us to focus our attention on certain areas because He knows where our testimony is needed most.

COMFORT ZONE 3: OUTSIDE RACIAL BOUNDARIES

Jesus told the disciples to witness in Jerusalem, Judea, and then Samaria. I believe this represents our need to witness beyond racial boundaries.

First-century Jews and Samaritans hated and despised one another. This is why the woman at the well with whom Jesus spoke about living water was so amazed that He even acknowledged her presence (John 4). The gospel of Jesus Christ must be shared with those whose skin color is different than ours. It must be shared with those whose culture and ethnic backgrounds are different than ours. It must be shared with those whose hair styles, body piercings, and choice in clothes are different than ours. People with tattoos and eyebrow rings need to hear about Jesus. We may not approve of their exterior appearance, but that does not limit their internal value.

I'm always amazed at our mind-set when we set out to do street evangelism. Almost 99.9 percent of the time we choose areas that are poverty stricken, as if to suggest no rich and affluent doctors, lawyers, engineers, and accountants need to know Christ. Samaria represents those opportunities the Lord gives us to share Him with people who may not be a part of our comfortable social environment. Jesus loved us enough to come to earth and intermingle with guilty, filthy sinners like you and me, who did not look or act like Him. We must do the same and express His love for all people, as well.

COMFORT ZONE 4: THE ENDLESS EXTENT

Jesus concludes with "… and to the end of the earth." God does not call everyone to witness for Him in foreign countries. But He has called all of us to witness about Him everywhere we go. Often our jobs require us to travel to some places we would not typically go. While we are there fulfilling our work responsibilities, we must not overlook the chance to introduce a person to Jesus Christ. Our responsibility to take our witness to the end of the earth could include our vacation time, our travels to visit with distant family and friends, and even those times when we find ourselves in unfamiliar surroundings, perhaps only a few miles from our homes.

If we are going to be witnesses who please the Lord, we must reach beyond our comfort zones, and depend, not on our intellect, but on the power of the Holy Spirit that will equip us to meet every challenge and pass every test to the glory of God.

A WORD FOR PASTORS AND LEADERS

It is extremely important for every pastor to establish some growth goals for his church and for every leader to establish some growth goals for his or her ministries. Your growth goals must not only include numerical advancement but also the people you plan to use within your congregation to help you to reach these goals, as well as the areas you will target. If we aim at nothing, we will hit it every time.

Setting goals also requires you to evaluate your effectiveness as an organizer. We must lead by example. We cannot expect a ministry to grow if we are not projecting a spirit of excellence in our leadership skills, or if we are not utilizing all the Lord Jesus has made available to us.

If you are not experiencing the growth you think pleases God, then take a moment and ask yourself how much witnessing you are doing in your Jerusalem. What about the Judea around you? When was the last time you shared Christ with someone who was of a different cultural or socio-economic background?

Of course, beyond witnessing, we need to develop and implement a discipleship plan if we are going to develop new converts into becoming quality kingdom citizens. Your growth goals must also include a plan to feed new believers and train them to share their testimony with others. If we fail to do this, new growth can lead to anarchy rather than Christian discipleship. Ask God to give you the faith to embrace His plan before you ask Him to trust you with new people!

10

Waiting on God in the Dark

Then Saul arose from the ground, and when his eyes were opened he saw no one. But they led him by the hand, and brought him into Damascus. And he was three days without sight, and neither ate nor drank.

ACTS 9:8–9

D oes God move too slowly? Sometimes we think so, and that's when we run ahead of Him to pursue what we desire from Him, or we procrastinate and fail to obey His Word. We have a "microwave" mentality and a "get it all now" disposition.

However, God has made some tremendous promises that reward those who patiently wait on Him. One of the most profound and beloved is found in Isaiah 40:31: "Those who wait on the Lord shall renew their strength; they shall mount up with wings like eagles, they shall run and not be weary, they shall walk and not faint."

We are by nature impulsive and impatient creatures, and we tend to expect quick results and instant relief, especially when we're in the midst of pain and suffering. But I have discovered that one of the hardest lessons for those of us who make up the community of Christian believers to learn is this: God does operate or move according to our timetable. We have difficulty both understanding and accepting that God knows when to move, how to move, whom to move, and where to move. So until He moves, the best thing we can do is to keep still and wait on Him.

Now, allow me to add a disclaimer here. When I use the phrase "keep still," I am not suggesting that we sit down, do nothing, and watch the world go by. I am saying that whatever problem or dilemma may be confronting us, we are responsible to keep doing what the Lord has called us to do, and to know beyond a shadow of a doubt that in His own good time He will either deliver us out of the situation, change the situation, or give us grace to handle the situation.

I have also come to realize that it is not always the situation that needs changing. More often we need to make a change in the situation and rest in the truth that God will give us grace to handle and accept whatever confronts us.

A prime example of this can be found in Paul's testimony when he said in 2 Corinthians 12:8–9, "Concerning this thing I pleaded with the Lord three times that it might depart from me. And He said to me, 'My grace is sufficient for you, for my strength is made perfect in weakness.' Therefore most gladly I will rather boast in my infirmities, that the power of Christ may rest upon me." This is what we call finding grace in strange places. Paul admits here that at his weakest hour God gave him a magnanimous portion of His grace. We will never receive all that the Lord has for us until we learn how to patiently and confidently wait on Him.

Now, it seems to be difficult enough for most of us to wait on God when the lights are on, the sun is shining, and we have 20/20 vision. But life has a way of causing us to face some predicaments that are accompanied by cloudy and uncertain elements. This story in Acts 9 informs us of a man who would become one of this world's greatest preachers, save Jesus Christ. He was forced to wait on God in the dark. The earlier chapters of Acts tell us Saul was a persecutor of the Lord's church. He was present at the stoning death of Stephen, one of the church's first seven deacons. Even though Saul did not participate in the stone throwing, Acts 7:58 tells us that he held the garments of those who threw the stones. Saul was being used by satan to cause tremendous havoc in the church of Jesus Christ. He was arresting Christians and putting them into prison simply because they were calling on and preaching in the name of Jesus Christ.

He had heard about some synagogues in Damascus, so he went to the high priest and got written approval from him to go there and bind anyone who was calling on the name of Jesus Christ. But on that day, much to his surprise, while on his way to the synagogues, he had a confrontation that changed his life for the rest of his life.

While traveling on that road to Damascus he was ambushed by a blinding light from heaven and knocked off his beast. He fell to the ground, and Jesus stopped him cold with the words, "Saul, Saul, why are you persecuting Me?"

> **Sometimes God uses dramatic methods to get our wholehearted and undivided attention.**

In some instances God chooses to knock us down from the high horses of our pride, egotism, selfish aggrandizement, and even the false comfort we receive from materialistic prosperity. God will do whatever is necessary to bring our lives in line with His will. I have found that God often uses these methods to save us from self-destruction.

On this day Saul was confronted with the truth that persecuting and mistreating the church of Christ is tantamount to persecuting and mistreating Jesus Himself. The church is the body of Christ, and whatever we do to His body we also do to Him.

On that Damascus road the persecutor met the Prince of peace, the garment holder met the Grace giver, the slaughterer met the Savior, the binder of believers met the One who blesses believers, the church fighter met the Church builder, and the prison taker met the Peacemaker. When Saul heard the voice of Jesus, he trembled and was astonished. Then he said, "Lord, what do You want me to do?" In other words, he was asking, "Lord, in which direction must I travel, and where do I go from here?" And Jesus answered, "Arise and go into the city, and you will be told what you must do" (Acts 9:6). Verse 8 says, "Then Saul arose from the ground, and when his eyes were opened he saw no one." Saul knew God had special plans for his life, but he did not know what those plans were.

Perhaps you are at this point in your ministry. You seem to be blinded from seeing God's perfect will, and you need to know where to begin to have your spiritual sight restored. A great place to start is to learn the importance of obeying the commands of God.

OBEYING THE COMMANDS OF GOD

Notice, Jesus gave to Paul in verse 6 what I call a specific command without any specifics to the command. He said to get up, go into the city, and I'll tell you later what I want you to do. In other words, go on into town and wait on Me to give you future instructions.

Sometimes the Lord gives us specific commands with specifics to the commands—like the one He gave to His disciples in Luke 22:10–12. He told them to go into the city and they would find a man bearing a pitcher of water. They were to follow him into whatever house he entered and tell him the Master needed the guest chamber for the Passover. Then they were told they would find a large upper room already furnished where they were to make ready for the Passover right there. That is an example of a specific command with specifics to the command.

Other times God purposefully gives us a specific command without any specifics to the command—like the one He gave to Abraham to pull up and leave Chaldea, his homeland, and kinsmen, and He would show him a city whose builder and maker was God. The only traveling directions

Abraham received were, essentially, I'll let you know you're there when you get there.

The Lord Jesus told Saul, in essence, I know you are blind, you are in the dark, you don't know anything about My mercy and grace. I know your pride is hurt, your ego has taken a nosedive, but if you are going to do great things for Me in the future, you must start by obeying My commands even in the dark.

Perhaps one of the most difficult lessons for us to learn and especially to apply is to trust God's heart even when we cannot trace His hand. We must obey Him even when we don't understand Him. We must surrender to Him even when we cannot see Him. He commanded Saul, "Go into the city," but He promised, "and you will be told what you must do." God may be speaking to you this very moment concerning your need to go where you can clearly hear His voice. He will never place new assignments before us until we acquiesce to His control.

God may not be leading you to a different geographical location. Some of us need to go to a new place of responsibility and accountability. Some of us need to go to a new place of intimacy with God. Some of us need to go to a new place of love and support toward our families. Whatever those places are, God is faithful to lead us there if we will capitulate to His will and obey His voice.

Saul, however, faced one major problem: he was blind. Also, he did not know how long he would have to wait in the city before he would receive his sight or get his marching orders. I am sure many of us can identify with this because we say we are willing to wait on God, but then we ask, "Lord, how long do I have to wait?" The blinding of Saul turned out to be a blessing in disguise. God used it to actually rearrange his agenda. He was on his way to Damascus with persecution on his mind, but when he got to Damascus he had preaching the gospel on his mind.

> The Lord reserves the right to send blinding and dark circum-
> stances in our lives because He works through them to teach us
> the value of reassessing our priorities and relying solely on Him.

If Saul had kept his sight, he may have tried to get back on his horse and ride away from Jesus. But there he was, flat on his back, in the dark, and all he could do was say, "Lord, what would You have me to do?"

God allows those conditions to manifest in our lives also. When we find ourselves hemmed in, backed up, broken down, with tear-stained faces and bleeding hearts, God waits for us to cry out, "Lord, what would You have me to do?" During those times He informs us that He does not care what we have planned. If our plans do not coincide with His plans, then He has the power to stop us, blind us, and to teach us how to wait on Him even in the dark. The only way we will ever regain our spiritual sight is to obey the commands of God even when they appear to be inexplicable and virtually impossible.

When I read this passage, I had one major concern: Saul was blind. How on earth would he be able to go into the city without his eyesight? I thank God I didn't stop reading with the first half of verse 8. That verse concludes by saying, "But they led him by the hand and brought him into Damascus." Wow! This lifted my heart tremendously. It helped me understand that when we obey the commands of God, He will also perfectly position someone who will allow us to observe the compassion of God.

OBSERVING THE COMPASSION OF GOD

When Saul arose from the ground, this represented his obedience to the command of God. Then God had people in place to take him by the hand into Damascus. The Lord had arranged for some people to be around him who would express what real godly compassion is all about. When we are waiting on God in the dark He not only gives us commands, but He also provides compassion.

I don't mean to be redundant here, but I must drive home this truth: "They led him by the hand and brought him into Damascus." They did not drag him, push him, or send him to Damascus. They took him by the hand. My personal relationship with the Lord has taught me that when we are faithfully waiting on God in the dark, He never forgets about us nor forsakes us. He always makes sure we have somebody to take us by the hand and lead us on just a little bit farther.

The problem many people in the family of God face is the issue of pride. Pride causes us to choose to stumble in the darkness of our own experiences rather than accept the hand God has made available to lead us out of the darkness. That "hand" can come in many forms.

The helping hand that leads us to our destination is not always a human hand. Sometimes our helping hand comes in the form of a Sunday school lesson, a sermon, a song of praise, or a Bible lesson. This is God's way of reminding us that we don't need 20/20 vision to see His compassion. God uses this method to allow our souls and spirits to become sensitive to observing the compassion of God.

That is what David was talking about when he said in Psalm 23:4, "Yea, though I walk through the valley of the shadow of death, I will fear no evil; for You are with me; Your rod and Your staff, they comfort me." Even when we face the lowest points in our lives, God's hand of compassion is right there. When we are hedged in by a seemingly impossible situation, when our resources appear to be depleted, we can go on knowing that the Lord is right with us every step of the way. God loves us enough to allow us to feel His compassion through another person.

Our God is a compassionate God. He comforts us when we are lonely, He guides us when we are lost, He holds us when we are trembling,

He forgives us when we pray, He catches us when we are falling, He corrects us when we are straying, He consoles us when we are burdened, and He welcomes us when we repent, turn around, and come back to Him.

Maybe you are wondering why things are the way they are in your life or ministry, why you're facing so much pain and uncertainty. And it seems as though help is extremely slow in arriving. Saul's experience is proof positive that even in our dark, blinding circumstances, God will never leave us without His love and protection.

There is one final principle I want to share from verse 9. There we read Saul "was three days without sight, and neither ate nor drank." After obeying the command from God to arise, and observing the compassion of God through the helping hands of others, Saul then displays his overwhelming commitment to God.

OVERWHELMING COMMITMENT TO GOD

When we read in verse 9 that Saul was without sight for three days, we know that was an act of God. But not eating or drinking for three days was a conscious decision he made on his own. Saul was an orthodox Jew, so he knew the spiritual significance of fasting. Though he could not see with his eyes, he was taking stock of the situation, and every hour the optical condition of his heart got closer and closer to God.

Saul did not know how long his blindness would last, but he did know Jesus had protected him thus far—even though he deserved to be wiped off the face of the earth. His determination to neither eat nor drink for three days is a display of his purging those physical things from his life to be filled with spiritual strength for his soul.

Sometimes we find ourselves waiting on God for direction and clarity.

Those seasons must be filled with an increased amount of fasting and quality prayer. We need to give up everything that hinders us if we really want God to turn our situation around.

Saul waited on God in the dark, and the Lord did not let him down. The Lord spoke to a man named Ananias and told him to go down to Straight Street to Judas's house where he would find Saul praying. When we can't do anything else, we should always pray, even in the dark.

Ananias obeyed the Lord even though reluctantly (I will say more about this in the following chapter), and God honored Saul's sacrifice and submission to Him.

When you take inventory of your life and ministry, you may find them filled with blind spots and darkness, but the good news is, God does some of His best work in the dark.

- It was dark when He spoke this world into existence.
- It was dark when He led the children of Israel across the Red Sea.
- It was dark when God gave Israel a pillar of fire by night.
- It was dark when God gave the Ten Commandments to Moses.
- It was dark when Jacob wrestled with the angel.
- It was dark when Moses instituted the Passover.
- It was dark when Daniel lay down and slept with lions.
- It was dark when the angel appeared to Mary.
- It was dark when the angels said, "Glory to God in the highest, and on earth peace, goodwill toward men" (Luke 2:14).
- It was dark when Nicodemus heard Jesus say, "You must be born again" (John 3:7).
- It was dark when Jesus gave the Lord's Supper.
- It was dark when Jesus prayed in the Garden of Gethsemane.
- It was dark when Jesus was marched from judgment hall to judgment hall.

- It was dark when Jesus hung on Calvary from the sixth to the ninth hours.
- It was dark when He died for our sins at Calvary. After three days in a dark grave, God allowed the sun to shine and the Son to rise, early on that first Easter Sunday morning.

Maybe your blindness has been caused by some act of disobedience or some unforeseen difficulty. Whatever the case, God's grace is able to repair us, restore us, and forgive us when we surrender to His will and submit to His authority.

A WORD FOR PASTORS AND LEADERS

At times we seem to be at our wits' end concerning God's will for our lives, churches, and ministries. This chapter gives us hope. God will never leave us in an area of vagueness and uncertainty without a date of deliverance and a purpose behind it all. Often He allows those periods to arise in our lives because He wants us to focus more on Him than on the assignments.

Successes in assignments have a way of inflating our egos and developing into selfish aggrandizement. But blindness has a way of teaching us total dependence and reliance upon God. No matter how complex the struggle may seem now, God has prepared someone to take you by the hand and lead you to the place where He desires you and your ministry to be.

God used one group of men to lead Saul into Damascus and another man to remove the scale-like objects from his eyes. This was God's way of getting other people involved in the initial stages of Saul's ministry. He met some people from whom he would never have experienced God's love if not for his blindness and being humbled by Jesus Christ.

Do you sense a season of blindness in your life? Fast and pray, and then wait on God to send His person to lead you out of it. Be patient and trust His timing—even if you have to wait on Him in the darkness.

11

Helping the Blind to See:
You Can Be an Ananias

*Now there was a certain disciple at Damascus named
Ananias; and to him the Lord said in a vision, "Ananias."
And he said, "Here I am, Lord." So the Lord said to him, "Arise
and go to the street called Straight, and inquire at the house of
Judas for one called Saul of Tarsus, for behold, he is praying.
And in a vision he has seen a man named Ananias coming in
and putting his hand on him, so that he might receive his sight."
Then Ananias answered, "Lord, I have heard from many about
this man, how much harm he has done to Your saints in
Jerusalem. And here he has authority from the chief priests to
bind all who call on Your name." But the Lord said to him,
"Go, for he is a chosen vessel of Mine to bear My name before
Gentiles, kings, and the children of Israel. For I will show him
how many things he must suffer for My name's sake." And
Ananias went his way and entered the house; and laying his
hands on him he said, "Brother Saul, the Lord Jesus who
appeared to you on the road as you came, has sent me that
you may receive your sight and be filled with the Holy Spirit."
Immediately there fell from his eyes something like scales,
and he received his sight at once; and he arose and was
baptized.*
ACTS 9:10–18

𝐻elen Keller was asked on one occasion, "What could be worse than being born blind?" Her response was "To have sight, and no vision for your life." So with that thought in mind, I want to begin this chapter by saying that most of us will never experience the fame and the notoriety of the apostle Paul, whose name was changed from Saul. The mistake many of us make is failing to excel where God has located us and not blossoming where God has planted us. In many instances the devil has deceived us into believing that just because we are not considered to be outstanding personalities in the kingdom of God, then our role in Christianity must be classified as humdrum, insignificant, and inoculated with a meaningless maze of mediocrity. This incident in Acts 9 helps us to recognize that the exact opposite is true.

Many of us overlook the fact that there are always people in the background who help those in the forefront to be all God would have them to be. Every football running back needs a good offensive line to block for him. Every basketball shooting guard needs good forwards and a center to rebound, play defense, and support him. God has structured the body of Christ to allow every person who has the responsibilities of an apostle Paul to see their need to be ministered to by an Ananias. These support people are there to lay hands and remove the scale-like objects that have blinded the leaders and kept them from seeing clearly what God wants to do in and with them.

Churches, and the kingdom of God as a whole, need more people like Ananias. We need those who are willing to be used by God to help us leaders with our human touch, who have already been touched by Him through heavenly salvation.

> We need more people willing to serve as intercessors
> to help those who have recently accepted Christ to
> know we are an extension of God's love.

We do not need more soloists. We need more altos, tenors, sopranos, and basses. We need more deacons, not more chairmen. We don't need more pastors, but more preachers to help the work of the church flow smoothly. We need more workers, not more supervisors. Ananias represents those whom God wants to use to help others discover their untapped talent, hidden potential, and unrealized gifts; those whom God wants to use to give people hope for the future and develop responsibilities in their present relationship with Christ. Ananias represents those whose names may never be called, whose faces may never be recognized, and who will never receive a star on Hollywood Boulevard, but who will receive a starry crown in heaven. Ananias represents the church van driver who makes sure people get to church and back home safely, the outreach group that goes to pray for the sick and offers assistance without being asked. He represents the Sunday school teacher who has only eight students but remains timely, faithful, and prepared each Sunday. Ananias represents the person who is on a fixed income yet faithfully pays the Lord twenty or twenty-five dollars each week, while strong able-bodied people who have been blessed by God with good jobs rob the Lord of the tithe week after week. Ananias represents the person who brings the thirsty a cup of water, who picks up trash around the church, who volunteers to work in a ministry without being asked—all because they see a need and know God wants to use them to do more than simply come to church and go back home after the benediction.

If we are going to help the blind to see—and I am speaking of those who are spiritually blind—then we need less folk who say, "I want to be like Mike," and more folk who will say "I want to be used like Ananias."

I see one prominent factor in this story that prevents many of us from being used as Ananias was. He was a "reluctant participant."

Did you know the church is still filled with reluctant participants? Most of us have already decided how far we are willing to go, how much we are willing to do, how much we are willing to give, and how often we are willing to talk about God. When He takes us out of our comfort zone and presents us with a new challenge, we start making excuses. Just like Ananias, we start telling God how little we know about the situation, completely ignoring the fact that He knows everything about the situation.

Let's look at three obstacles to becoming like Ananias.

Verses 13 and 14 say, "Ananias answered, 'Lord, I have heard from many about this man, how much harm he has done to Your saints in Jerusalem. And here he has authority from the chief priests to bind all who call on Your name.'"

Most of don't want to be like Ananias because doing so would force us to deal with some unfriendly people.

UNFRIENDLY PEOPLE

Notice Ananias's initial complaint: "Lord, I have heard from many about this man, how much harm he has done to Your saints." The word *harm* literally means bad things. Ananias had heard about Saul's past hurtful and antagonistic activities. In the past he was vile, repugnant, gross, immoral, despicable, rude, vicious, violent, a "hater" of the brethren, a cruel manifestation of creation, a man void of compassion, denuded of respect, and infested with a cantankerous posture of destruction. Saul had done some bad things.

Many of us don't talk about Jesus to people who are lost because they are unfriendly, and we know about their past negative activity. We have heard about their adultery, their time in prison, or the abortion before they accepted Christ. However, we all have some failures in our past, and if we are going to grow our churches and help to populate the kingdom of God, we must be willing to interact with what we may consider to be unfriendly people.

Something else about this text really stands out as a problem, not only for Ananias, but also for many of us. Ananias knew what Saul had done in the past, but he was not aware of what God had done in the present. Many of us can see clearly the difficulties of the past, but we overlook God's hand at work right now. We need to know that whenever and wherever God sends us, we can always be assured of His provisions and His protection.

We also need to understand that in some instances God will send us to unfriendly people so we can witness firsthand the change He has made in their lives. Many of us never see the change because our fears cause us to focus only on the bad in their past.

Now notice how God responds to Ananias in verse 15: "But the Lord said to him, 'Go, for he is a chosen vessel of Mine to bear My name before Gentiles, kings, and the children of Israel.'"

Then verse 17 tells us, "Ananias went his way and entered the house." Our being used by God like Ananias also includes being willing and available to go to some unfamiliar places.

UNFAMILIAR PLACES

After Ananias finished complaining in verse 14, God's response went something like this: "I told you to go in verse 11, and I'm still telling you to go right now." When God gives us a command, it is not up for discussion or debate. We know God prepared Saul to receive Ananias, and God was preparing Ananias to embrace Saul. God did to Saul in verses 3–9 what only God could do. God was saying to Ananias, "I want you to do what I have equipped you to do and to travel in the direction I am sending you." For the Christian life is filled with challenges and we, like Ananias, must not shrink back when God wants to send us to some unfamiliar places to bring glory and honor to Him.

Throughout the Word of God, every great man and woman of God had to go to some unfamiliar places for their faith to be developed.

Abraham left Chaldea looking for Canaan and there he found the Promised Land. Jacob left Canaan headed to Paddan Aram. Joseph left Canaan, having been sold as a slave, but in Egypt God elevated him to the position of prime minister. Moses left Egypt and went to the backside of the desert, where he met God and was used by Him to lead Israel out of evil Egyptian captivity. Joshua left the wilderness and entered back into Canaan. The Hebrew boys went into the unfamiliar place known as Babylon and discovered God's ability to deliver them from a fiery furnace. Daniel also discovered in the unfamiliar place of Babylon God's ability to deliver him from a den of lions. Job went from great riches to the unfamiliar place of abject poverty, and God gave him "double for his trouble" after he prayed for his friends. Esther went to the unfamiliar place of going before the king without an appointment, and God used her to save her people. Mary went to the unfamiliar place of pregnancy without physical intimacy with a man, and she brought forth the only begotten Son of God. All of these biblical examples help us to realize we can handle unfamiliar places.

The Lord may be asking you to heed His voice, remove yourself from a comfort zone, and travel with Him to an unfamiliar place. Perhaps your unfamiliar place may be ministry leadership or active involvement in a ministry. It may include leaving the church you attend with your family and friends only because of your allegiance to them rather than for your spiritual growth. It may include a commitment to increased giving. Or, as is in this text, God may desire to use you to represent Him to a person who has a terrible past.

Wherever God is leading you, obey and follow Him by faith and watch God work a miracle through you.

Verse 17 tells us that after Ananias laid his hands on Saul, he told Saul he had been sent by the Lord to restore his sight and lead him into being filled with the Holy Spirit. Then verse 18 says, "Immediately there fell from his eyes something like scales." God's challenge to Ananias included ministering to a previously unfriendly person and going to an unfamiliar place. Once he obeyed the Lord, however, Ananias discovered he had some unrealized power.

UNREALIZED POWER

When I first read this, a big smile came to my face. I believe that when those scale-like objects fell from Saul's eyes, Ananias was more surprised than Saul! Most of us will never see hindrances fall from people's eyes, because we fail to make ourselves available for God to do the impossible through us. The Lord wants us to know that if we are His children, then His power is already in us. All He wants us to do is to realize it and release it! God never sends us to a ministry assignment to set us up for failure. There will be difficulties, uncertainties, and even disappointments. But these are simply tools God uses to teach us about His ability to do through us what we never could have dreamed possible on our own.

Even while we were watching the vision God had given to me for the Grace Tabernacle Church come to pass, one scale-like object after another stood before us. Yet God always sent someone to encourage us and remove those things from our path. We pressed on while the building costs were increasing, but God would send grace givers and those scales would fall off. The demands of ministry were increasing, but God sent committed leaders and workers and those scales fell off.

When we keep touching people for God, walking in the faith of God, and trusting God even when it seems like it will not work out, God will allow scales of hindrances to fall off.

God will allow scales to fall from preachers' eyes, and we will preach the Word with more power. God will allow scales to fall from deacons' eyes, and they will serve with more power. God will allow scales to fall from choir members' eyes, and they will sing with more power. God will allow scales to fall from ushers' eyes, and they will stand with more power.

The scale-like objects fell from Saul's eyes because Ananias laid his hands on him, and I believe we all have the God-given power to touch people for God and help them see God's will for their lives. We all know someone who is blinded by being unchurched or unsaved. We all know someone who was active in a local congregation but now sits idly by every Sunday. We all know people who feel hopeless and helpless and don't know where to turn. The Lord wants us to follow the pattern of Ananias, even if it means going to their homes and touching them on His behalf.

The touch represents God's love, care, and compassion for them. We can touch them with our words and His message, and tell them He is faithful, forgiving, and fathering. We can share with them that He is mighty, merciful, and matchless. We can explain to them that He wipes out yesterday, gives a fresh start on today, and provides a brighter outlook for tomorrow. We can express to them that He is not only the God of a second chance, but a third, fourth, or fifth chance. God can use us to fill every pew in our churches. He wants each of us to make it our business to never come to worship alone again. You may not ever lead the ministry, but God can use you to reach the Saul who will lead and give Him glory.

Perhaps you wonder, "If God wants to use me to win people like Saul, then why does it seem so difficult to understand His will for my life?" The answer to that question can be found in Acts 9:16, where Jesus said, "For I will show him how many things he must suffer for My name's sake." Many of us cannot handle leadership responsibilities because we cannot handle the suffering that goes along with them.

In verse 18 we read that Saul was baptized after the scale-like objects fell from his eyes. He was then able to see and serve, and because of Ananias's obedience the gospel was preached by Paul throughout much of the world of that day. At least thirteen letters of the New Testament were written by him, and thousands of souls were saved. It all began because God chose to use this inconspicuous man named Ananias to touch an *unfriendly person*, go to an *unfamiliar place*, use his *unrealized power*, and witness some *unbelievable participation*. Saul left his home three days prior, determined to destroy the church, but after this day, he spent all of his energy trying to develop the church.

And when scales start to fall from people's eyes, God can change

- pimps into preachers,
- dope-heads into deacons,
- child molesters into youth directors,
- street walkers into door-to-door evangelists,
- crack-heads into ministry leaders,
- alcoholics into Sunday school teachers, and
- church fighters into church builders.

Our prayer should be, "Lord, use me to help the blind to see."

A WORD FOR PASTORS AND LEADERS

We must never lose sight of the fact that God can bring about tremendous results through unlikely people. This very book is a testimony to that fact. Many people whom you will never meet have worked behind the scenes praying for me, encouraging me, and supporting me. They will never preach in a revival, facilitate a conference, or have their names on a church marquee. God has strategically positioned them in the body of Christ as enablers. We must welcome these precious people when we know God has sent them into our lives.

We will never be able to accomplish all God has for us if we remain in our blindness. Jesus spoke to Saul, Jesus spoke to Ananias, and they worked together to accomplish God's will. God used them as partners in ministry, and He can do the same today.

When your vision seems blinded or blurry, God is faithful to send an Ananias with His touch of encouragement into your life. Just like He chooses to speak to us through other people, He also chooses to touch us through other people. If you are experiencing a period of blindness in your church or ministry, God may be getting ready to use you like you have never been used by Him before!

12

The Difficulties of Discipleship

Now after many days were past, the Jews plotted to kill him.
But their plot became known to Saul. And they watched the gates
day and night, to kill him. Then the disciples took him by night
and let him down through the wall in a large basket.
Acts 9:23–25

One of the greatest mistakes many people make after surrendering their lives to Christ and becoming connected to a local church is to assume that all of their troubles and difficulties will vanish with some sort of spiritual hocus pocus. We think some magic wand will be waved, and from that day forward we will see nothing but sunshine and blue skies.

When we are born again and join a local church, the devil does not retreat from us. Rather, he repeatedly and viciously hounds us because he knows he has lost a member of his army. We fail to understand that Christianity is an arena for warfare. And as members of God's army, we need to be prepared to fight. This is precisely why Paul says in Ephesians 6:11, "Put on the whole armor of God, that you may be able to stand against the *wiles* of the devil." The word wiles means travesty, trickery, and to lie in wait with the intent to deceive and destroy. Paul was making us aware of how the devil will lie in wait to deceive us, dissuade us, and to discourage us from doing and becoming all God has for us. satan's plan against us begins as soon as we commit ourselves to Jesus Christ, and discipleship comes with difficulties.

Walking with Jesus is no leisurely stroll down a road of roses. It is no promenade down a path of peacefulness, nor is it an amble along Aromatic Avenue. When Jesus saved us, we became a threat to the devil. Satan knows the more we do for Jesus, the more we will do against him; and his influence in our lives will be greatly reduced. The devil became angry when we surrendered to Christ, became attached to a church family, and started tithing, testifying, and trusting. He is upset that we are now striving to walk faithfully, work fruitfully, and worship fully. He is troubled that we are now loving passionately, leading purposefully, and learning productively. And he will do everything he can to hinder our progress. But the good news is, "He who is in you is greater than he who is in the world" (1 John 4:4).

The apostle Paul knew that living for Jesus and talking about Jesus would not be easy. He knew this because the Lord told him through Ananias that he would be shown how many things he would suffer for Jesus' name's sake (Acts 9:16).

Very few of us like to discuss this matter of suffering. But the Bible says in Romans 8:17, "if indeed we suffer with Him, that we may also be glorified together." We can rejoice that suffering for Jesus is temporary, but reigning with Jesus is eternal.

The Bible tells us that after Saul was converted and blinded, he spent three days fasting. The Lord Jesus sent Ananias to lay hands on Saul, and then scale-like objects fell from his eyes. "Immediately he preached the Christ in the synagogues, that He is the Son of God" (Acts 9:20).

When we arrive at verse 23, we read some disheartening and discouraging information: "Now after many days were past, the Jews plotted to kill him." As we disciple others, we, too, can expect extreme opposition.

EXTREME OPPOSITION

If we are going to grow churches and ministries that glorify God, we can expect the devil to be relentless in his attacks against us. Before a football player takes the field, the coach and the trainer makes sure he has cleats on his feet, shoulder pads, shin guards, thigh pads, a helmet, a mouthpiece, and all the other necessary equipment. The player wears this equipment because he knows that once he gets into the game, the opposition may hit him anywhere at any time. He knows the opposition is prepared to hit him, so he needs to be prepared to handle the hits.

Many Christians are easily wounded in spiritual battles and carried off the field of holy service on stretchers. We fall because we are unable to handle the blows the devil hurls against our faith and productivity. This happens, first, because many of us don't show up for practice. (By *practice* I mean involvement in corporate prayer time, Bible study, church school, and ministries of our local churches.) Then when God gives the coach (the pastor) the authority to call a play for the advancement of the kingdom, we have no idea what he is talking about.

Second, we go through life uncovered, without the protection God has made available. Paul had a specific purpose in mind when he told us to put on the "whole" armor of God. He knew the devil would attack us every time he had an opportunity. Just like the owner of the football team provides equipment for His players, God provides equipment for His children. We have at least sixty-six pieces of equipment known as the sixty-six books in the Word of God. For example, the owner of our team (God) has authorized His Son Jesus Christ to provide for us the grace of Genesis, the energy of Exodus, the learning of Leviticus, the nourishment of Numbers, the discipline of Deuteronomy, the joy of Joshua, the justice of Judges. We have also been afforded the praise of Psalms, the education of Ecclesiastes, the insight of Isaiah, the deliverance of Daniel, and the mercy of Malachi.

Our equipment continues with the mission of Mark, the love of Luke, the justification of John, the action of Acts, the correction of Corinthians, the teachings of Timothy, the healing of Hebrews, and the rejoicing of Revelation. So the next time you feel beat up by the devil, it just may be because you have left all of your equipment sitting at home on your coffee table, on your night stand, or on the dashboard of your car.

Acts 9:23 says the Jews sought to kill Paul after many days were past. These "many days" turned out to be about three years that Paul refers to in Galatians 1:17–18. He spent this time in Arabia, and while he was there, at least three things took place that prepared him for ministry. These things are vital to our ministries as well.

1. SECLUSION

First of all, he spent some time in seclusion. He got away from his familiar surroundings. Most of us make the mistake of going back into the very thing from which God has just delivered us. We need to know that seclusion gives us an opportunity to spend some uninterrupted time with God away from television and other media, away from children and friends, and away from worldly responsibilities. When did you last turn off your cell phone just so you could spend some quality time in prayer and meditation with God? As a pastor, I observe cell phones ringing in worship, Bible study, prayer meeting, and ministry meetings. I even see people leave the sanctuary to engage in conversations, missing the preached Word that could provide much-needed liberation for their souls and spirits. But Paul was successful because he spent some time in seclusion with God.

2. STUDY

Second, he spent time in study of the Word of God. Our work for God will never surpass our knowledge of the Word of God. Many of us are unable to do more for God because we have a limited knowledge of His expectations from us and His promises to us. Paul's time alone in Arabia provided an opportunity for him to search the Scriptures and develop an intimate relationship with God. What regular discipline do you have to systematically study God's Word? If we are to grow, we must make time for God to speak to us through the Scriptures.

3. STABILITY

Third, Paul spent time developing his stability. Notice the trend of progression here. He was *secluded*, which provided an opportunity for him to study, and his *study* led to his *stability*. The second half of Acts 9:23 is still true today. The devil is still plotting to kill anybody who is attempting to do a great work for God. The only way you and I will be able to deal with the difficulties involved in discipleship is to remember the opposition is extreme, and we must prepare ourselves to deal with whatever the devil throws in our path.

Paul wrote in 1 Corinthians 15:58, "Therefore, my beloved brethren, be steadfast, immovable, always abounding in the work of the Lord, knowing that your labor is not in vain in the Lord." We should strive to exhibit a model of stability in Christ before the world.

Back in Acts 9, we read in verse 24, "But their plot became known to Saul. And they watched the gates day and night, to kill him." God not only equips us for extreme opposition, but He is also able to expose our opposition.

EXPOSE OPPOSITION

When we are truly pursuing God's will for our lives, He will reveal our real enemies. Many of us make the mistake of panicking, running, and hiding from our ministry responsibilities when we get word that trouble lies ahead. Paul's very life was being threatened, but most of us will quit if we get word that someone does not totally agree with us, or if someone has said or done something to hurt our feelings. We need to know that God is not as concerned about our feelings as He is about our faithfulness. Our feelings are deceiving, temporary, and fluctuating, but faithfulness is lasting, powerful, and productive.

Verse 24 gives us another principle for ministry. Saul learned of the plot to kill him, and the men constantly watched the gates for the perfect opportunity. They were watching the gates—but God was watching them, the gates, and Paul! They could only watch the gates.

This is why we need not spend time worrying about our enemies. While they are watching the gates, our God is watching us, them, and the gates. God knows how to warn us and direct us away from the enemy, and God always sends someone to us to lend us a helping hand in our time of need. This truth is confirmed in verse 25: "Then the disciples took him by night and let him through the wall in a large basket."

When we are loyal to and dependent on God, He preserves us in the midst of *extreme opposition*, He is able to *expose* our *opposition*, and He gives us the ability to *escape* our *opposition*.

ESCAPE OPPOSITION

"The Lord will make a way somehow!" Notice how God intervened in this situation. While the enemy was watching the gates, the main entrances of the city, God had arranged for Paul to escape through a wall, literally through a window and down a wall. Perhaps Paul was thinking of this experience when he wrote 1 Corinthians 10:13: "No temptation has overtaken you except such as is common to man; but God is faithful, who will not allow you to be tempted beyond what you are able, but with the temptation will also make the way of escape, that you may be able to bear it."

As I mentioned, my mother used to say, "He will never place more on you than you are able to bear" and "God will always make a way out."

God is able to bring us out. He is not limited in His ability. He can do it *collectively*. The Lord had other disciples in place to help Paul during this season of difficulty.

It was also a *calculated* escape. The Lord did it at night when perhaps they least expected it. God is able to set us free and leave our enemies wondering when it happened and how they missed it.

Paul's escape was also *comfortable*. His friends did not drop him down, they did not push him down, they did not make him jump down. They carefully let him down in a basket. Praise the Lord! God is not only able to allow us to escape *completely*, but He also allows us to escape comfortably. God will never allow us to be led into anything for His sake that He is not able to deliver us from. Our God is the God of a way out.

- He was a way out of the pit and out of the prison for Joseph.
- He was a way out of Egypt for Moses.
- He was a way out of adultery for David.
- He was a way out of poverty for Job.
- He was a way out of a lions' den for Daniel.
- He was a way out of a fiery furnace for the Hebrew boys.
- He was a way out of a big fish for Jonah.
- He was a way out of jail for Paul and Silas.

And when we needed a way out of our sins, Jesus switched roles. He came into to this world and got into Mary. He came into a lost humanity, died at Calvary, went into a grave, and early the third day, He came out of the tomb with all power in His hands.

God will bring you out, but not until He has finished developing you right where you are. So until then, just hold on and know that the Lord will make a way somehow.

A WORD FOR PASTORS AND LEADERS

We must brace ourselves in advance for the attacks we will certainly face. Not only must we prepare ourselves, but we must also be a strong source of encouragement to those who look to us for leadership.

The strategy of the enemy is twofold. First, he will seek to discourage us, especially when it appears all our genuine efforts are not producing the immediate fruit we desire.

Second, the enemy will seek to fill the minds of leaders who work under us with that same discouragement. If he is successful, the end result will be vacancies in ministry. If he cannot defeat the leader, he will launch an all-out assault on those who follow our leadership.

We must be encouraged as well as encouragers as we continue to develop new people for assignments and never lose sight of the facts that God will complete the work that He has started in us.

13

A Confrontation That Changed a Life

Immediately he preached the Christ in the synagogues, that He
is the Son of God. Then all who heard were amazed, and said,
"Is this not he who destroyed those who called on this name in
Jerusalem, and has come here for that purpose, so that he might
bring them bound to the chief priests?" But Saul increased all
the more in strength, and confounded the Jews who dwelt in
Damascus, proving that this Jesus is the Christ.
ACTS 9:20–22

There is nothing more precious or memorable for a Christian than to look back and see where we've come from and what God has brought us through. For some of us, this experience is filled with a greater degree of preciousness because we can remember the day and hour Jesus called us out of darkness and ushered us into His luminous light. Many of us can remember our confrontation with the Christ of Calvary when we turned our backs on the devil and our testimony became "I have decided to choose Jesus." We remember the tears that filled our eyes, the joy that flooded our hearts, the praise that flowed from our lips, the mercy that fixed our past, and the grace that framed our future. It is a wonderful thing to be able to look back over our lives and see the powerful hand of God at work in us and for us every step of the way.

Unfortunately, many people are not committed to making progress for the Lord because they have not taken the time to consider, contemplate, and appreciate how far God has brought them. Some people feel they are where they are because they know the right people or because someone pulled some strings for them. Still others feel they've "arrived" because of their accomplishments, intellectual astuteness, family lineage, or just because of a lucky break. But the truth is, we are where we are because of the grace of God.

In this chapter we will focus on the positive results of our captivating confrontation with the Christ of Calvary. I do not believe it is possible for us to come into personal contact with Jesus and leave His presence exactly the same. When we are confronted by Jesus we may leave Him with bitter rejection and obstinate hostility, which results from denial, doubt, and disbelief. We may even leave with a demonic disposition of negativity, thinking, "When I'm dead I'm done because nobody can do anything about my hopeless and helpless condition." Or, we may leave like many have, knowing there is a Savior for sinners, forgiveness for our faults, pardon for our past, protection for our pilgrimage, joy for our journey, deliverance from our disasters, and a bright side somewhere. In December of 1973, when I met Jesus, I left that confrontation more determined to do His will, assured of His provisions, and excited about His acceptance of me into His family in spite of my past hideous thoughts and deeds. I also discovered it was not enough for me to simply say, "The Lord has changed my life." Those words must be followed and accompanied by some positive and powerful activities that will ultimately bring glory and honor to the name of our resurrected Christ.

Paul shows us here in our text what our lives should look like, and what our actions should be, once we have had a captivating confrontation with Jesus Christ. This text forces us to examine ourselves and answer the question, "How serious am I about doing God's will and making myself available for Him to be glorified through my life?" Many of us have relegated ourselves to merely attending church and going through the motions of "ecclesiastical exercises" and "Christian calisthenics." We work up a sweat inside the church building, but we remain totally uninvolved after the benediction on the outside of the building. God wants total custody of His children, not just weekend visits.

The apostle Paul gives us a prime example in verses 20–22 of the evidences of a positive confrontation with Christ.

In verse 20 we read, "Immediately he preached the Christ in the synagogues, that He is the Son of God." Look at that first word: *immediately*. This was a rapid involvement.

RAPID INVOLVEMENT

After Paul's conversion, God used Ananias to cause the scale-like objects to fall from Paul's eyes. Acts 9:19 tells us Paul then did two things: He ate something for physical strength and spent some time with the disciples at Damascus for spiritual strength. Then he was immediately ready to go to work for the Lord.

Many of us cannot be as committed to the Lord as He would like us to be because we allow too many trivial matters to fill the time between our confrontation with Him and our working for Him.

Many people have been confronted by Him in an emotional worship experience on Sunday and then fail to return to His house until the next Sunday. But during the week we face the problems of lack of money on Monday, tough tests on Tuesday, worries on Wednesday, terrors on Thursday, fears on Friday, and sickness on Saturday. And by the time Sunday rolls back around, we are too mad to shout about anything, too tired to get involved in anything, too faithless to commit to anything, too broke to give anything, and too sad to rejoice over anything.

Our churches seem to be filled with procrastinators—those who postpone their involvement until next Sunday or next month. These people fail to realize that tomorrow is not promised to anyone. God is looking for what I like to call "immediate, right-now folk." He is doing great things in our lives right now, and He expects the same from us.

The Bible tells us that Paul started preaching immediately in the synagogues that Jesus is the Son of God. This prevented the devil from filling his mind and life with all kinds of negative thoughts and activities.

The pattern never fails. At Grace Tabernacle, those who start off right maintain greater, lasting, and positive devotion to the Lord and His church. Our involvement in the ministries of the church should be rapid. You need to get involved, and you need to do so in a hurry. I implore you to find a ministry today and make a commitment today. Get off the sideline right now. If you know God is being good to you right now, then become more committed to Him right now. If you are committed to Christ, then this should be your cry of encouragement to others who are uncommitted.

Verse 20 tells us about Paul's rapid involvement, and verse 21 tells us of his reversed intentions.

REVERSED INTENTIONS

The Bible tells us that when the people heard Paul was preaching the gospel, they were all amazed and said, "Is this not he who destroyed those who called on this name in Jerusalem, and has come here for that purpose, so that he might bring them bound to the chief priests?" These people were under the false assumption and the injudicious misconception that Paul's intentions remained unchanged. But they failed to realize something had happened to him on the Damascus road that reversed his intentions, rearranged his itinerary, restricted his influence, refocused his insight, and readjusted his importance. Likewise, when Jesus becomes real to you, you will experience a reversal of your intentions.

If you are thinking I am only referring to a reversal of intentions relative to church persecution, then you are sadly mistaken. We need to embrace the broader scope of this matter. Our intentions need to be reversed if we are approaching ministry involvement with the thought of remaining at our current level of commitment.

Your intentions need to be reversed if you are uninvolved and you plan to remain uninvolved. Many of us think we can justifiably hide behind the idea of "I am not a persecutor of the church like Saul was, so I don't need to change." Well, that's a belief we need to change.

I do not know a whole lot about human anatomy and chemistry, but I do know there are two ways the body can be destroyed, weakened, and harmed: by malicious physical attack or by purposeful neglect. The church is the body of Christ, and while people aren't necessarily attacking the church outright, the church is weak because people purposefully neglect it. The Sunday school is weak because people refuse to utilize their teaching skills. The giving is low in many churches because members refuse to pay the tithe. The prayer hour is weak because folks refuse to collectively place their adorations and petitions before God. These are all examples of a need for intentions to be reversed.

The people who heard Paul were amazed because God had made a noticeable change in Paul's life. We will never be all God would have us to be until we allow Him to completely reverse our intentions so that our lives will become testimonies of His great power.

Then, finally, verse 22 says, "But Saul increased all the more in strength, and confounded the Jews who dwelt in Damascus, proving that this Jesus is the Christ."

Paul experienced a rapid involvement in ministry, some reversed intentions toward ministry, and results that were irrefutable for ministry.

RESULTS THAT WERE IRREFUTABLE

When Paul obeyed God, the Lord rewarded him with some results that were irrefutable.

Four words caught my attention in verse 22: *increased*, *strength*, *confounded*, and *proving*.

INCREASED

Increased means to be empowered, to be made strong, and it is used only one time in the entire New Testament. When Paul made himself available to the Lord, God gave him more inner power than he ever dreamed possible— God "increased" his power. Many people sit back, thinking they do not have what it takes—and they're right! We cannot do it alone, but if we will offer God our availability, He will take care of the abilities.

STRENGTH

The second word is *strength*. This is what God gave Paul, and it means to be strategically positioned to use externally what God has given you internally. In other words, when we make ourselves available to the Lord, He not only gives us great power, but He also positions us in a great place to use the great power. God has placed you in that church or ministry because He has work for you to do right where you are. Countless individuals have not been able to display the power of God and bless the place where God has planted them because the devil has told them they don't have what takes, and they have believed his lie. In truth, we can do all things through Christ Jesus who strengthens us!

CONFOUNDED

The third word is *confounded*, and it means to perplex the mind, to baffle, and to totally mesmerize. When the Jews arrived at the synagogue, they expected to hear one thing coming out of Paul's mouth, but God allowed him to baffle and mesmerize them.

Have you ever seen a shy person who becomes willing to lead a song, teach a class, make a speech, or work with a ministry? After he or she totally makes him- or herself available to the Lord, he starts singing better than anybody expected, she teaches better than anybody expected, he speaks better than anyone expected, and she serves more faithfully than anyone expected. And people say, "I didn't know you had all of that in you." They have been totally mesmerized. These people didn't know Paul had all of this in him, either. But it all happened because he made himself available to the Lord. Now notice the progression of the words. *Increased* talks about what he had, *strength* deals with where he was to use what he had, and *confounded* deals with how he used what he had where he was. It all led to him *proving* that Jesus is the Christ.

PROVING

Proving means to weave and knit together, to unite affection with association. Paul had been given the ability by God to unite some Old Testament scholars with some of the eager new converts in his audience. So he started weaving together and uniting the fact that Jesus was the Old Testament Creator with the fact that He is the New Testament Christ. He was the Old Testament rod of Moses and He is the New Testament Rock for His disciples. He was the Old Testament water for the children of Israel, and He is the New Testament wine for guests at a wedding in Cana. He was the Old Testament lifeguard for Jonah, and He is the New Testament life God for Peter. He was the Old Testament fire of power for Elijah on Mount Carmel, but thank God He is our New Testament Sacrifice of Perfection on Mount Calvary.

When we have had a personal confrontation with Him we can tell the world

- He is a Designer and Deliverer.
- He is our Shadow and our Substance.
- He is our Help in ages past, and He is our Hope for years to come.
- He is our Escape from hell, and He is our Escort into heaven.
- He is our Instructor and our Inspiration.
- He is our Father and He is our Friend.
- He is our Producer and He is our Protection.
- He is our Commander and He allows us to be His co laborers.
- He is our Kinsman and He is our King!

A WORD FOR PASTORS AND LEADERS

One things that has brought a tremendous amount of peace and balance to my life and ministry has been my willingness to surrender the need to prove myself to others. God has shown to me that when I give Him my best, the work He does through me will speak for itself. Often we become stressed over what others will think of us and how they will evaluate us, while we fail to seek God's approval and His stamp of endorsement.

Paul did not allow others' thoughts or expectations of him to hinder him from fulfilling what he knew God had called him to do. Likewise, God has not called us to appease people or to win their favor, but He has called us to serve them. You will experience times of struggle in ministry when others seem to be blossoming and becoming more fruitful than you are. But you may be unaware of the many others who wish to God they had what He has trusted you with.

If your life has been confronted by and changed positively for God, then make yourself totally available and watch God amaze people around you with the quality of ministry He produces through you. If you focus on giving God the glory in your ministry, He will give you the grace for your ministry.

14

A Message from the Matchless Man in the Middle

They crucified Him, and two others with Him, one on either side, and Jesus in the center.
JOHN 19:18

In John 2, we read about Jesus and His disciples attending a wedding feast in Cana of Galilee. While they were there, Mary informed her Son that they had run out of wine. Jesus then performed His first miracle by changing water into wine. After the governor of the feast had tasted the new miraculous wine, he commented, essentially, "You have saved the best for last."

We have now come to the final chapter, and I, too, have saved the best for last. I'm not suggesting the information in this chapter will be superior or more valuable than the material in previous chapters. Rather, I'm emphasizing that if it had not been for the ultimate "Man in the Middle"—Jesus Christ—we could not share and would not need to receive what has been distributed up to this point.

As a young preacher I was taught by our elder pastors the importance of never ending a sermon until we had strongly emphasized the death, burial, and resurrection of Jesus Christ. I have also sought to follow that advice in the writing of this book. If you have spent any time in an African American worship experience, you are perhaps familiar with how most of us who preach the gospel of Jesus Christ never conclude our sermons until we shout the words with spiritual excitement, "He died, didn't He die!" His sacrificial act at Calvary is the apex and the panacea of our faith. Without it, His life would be relegated to that of just another great orator, philosopher, or moralist.. Those of us who enjoy a personal and intimate relationship with Jesus Christ know that His life means so much more than these temporary superficial titles would suggest.

He is our Creator; He manifested that element of His personality when He made us in His own image.

He is our Savior; He manifested that element of His personality when He died at Calvary for us.

Today, He lives in us through the Holy Spirit as He leads us, guides us, and gives us the power and ability to fulfill everything He has assigned us to do.

Thus, our final area of focus here will be on His love for us and His willingness to surrender His life to evil men through death on a cross for the sins of the whole world. Jesus has made His blood and His forgiveness available for everyone who will accept it.

John 19:17 tells us Jesus was crucified on Golgotha. We refer to it today as Calvary. Golgotha was a skull-shaped hill known as the place of death. Little did the executioners of Jesus realize how He was about to transform a place that epitomized death into a place that would come to symbolize eternal life. This is indicative of the entire life and ministry of Jesus. He was able to reduce to worthlessness those things people valued highly, and elevate to pricelessness those things people considered worthless. This is one reason Christians refer to the Friday Jesus was crucified as "Good Friday." That bloody, gruesome, and pain-filled day became our day of redemption, restoration, and reconciliation. He did not have to die for us; He freely offered Himself. He was not forced to give His life; He did so freely. He had power to defend Himself, but He chose to save us by paying a debt He did not owe because He knew we owed a debt we could not pay.

When we even attempt to understand why Jesus did this for us, we discover how completely incomprehensible His actions were. His sacrifice for us is not only ultimate and supreme, it is also mind-boggling and indescribable. He had absolutely nothing to gain by subjecting Himself to dehumanizing pain at the hands of evil men. All we can say is that His love for us far exceeds our ability to comprehend or deserve the astounding forfeiture of His physical life on that bloody and pain-filled Friday.

We view sacrifice from a human vantage point, and we always assume some personal gain. We sacrifice for others because of what they have already done for us or because of what we are hoping they will do for us, but this was not the case with Jesus. All of our actions caused Him harm, pain, and disgrace. Isaiah tells us we are no better than filthy rags even at our best. With this in mind, I want to share with you what the Holy Spirit shared with me concerning how Jesus was able to fill His role as the ultimate "Man in the Middle" so effectively.

Jesus was able to do all He did for us because He not only wanted to be the perfect sacrifice for us, but He also wanted us to represent Him effectively after He was gone. He displays this in at least three prominent arenas.

1. HE WAS CONSCIOUS OF OUR SINFUL CONDITION

Our sinful condition was no surprise to Jesus when He arrived on earth; He did not come with a set of unrealistic expectations. This speaks to at least two additional positive characteristics about Jesus: First, He loved us enough to come and save us, knowing full well our depraved condition; second, He came knowing we would be unable to live lives of perfection even after we were saved because of the presence of sin in our world.

Many of us fail to realize that Jesus not only loved us enough to save us from sin, but He also continues to love us after our salvation when we yield to the temptation of sin. He knew then and He knows now about all our imperfections. He was not blindsided by the condition of our souls. He was completely aware of the mess satan had made of our lives. He came here to die for us, to shed every drop of His blood for the remission of our sins. He did not have an alternate plan. He knew Calvary would be the once-and-for-all remedy for our alienated condition from God.

We will never be effective witnesses for our Christ until we realize that when we seek to win the lost for Him, we are approaching people whose lives have been marred and blemished by the power of evil. We cannot overlook them, because Jesus came to save sinners.

We must also remember there are no different classes of sinners. Romans 3:23 says, "All have sinned and fall short of the glory of God." There are no degrees of being unsaved; there is only heaven and hell. We will never be successful as His witnesses until we recognize the sinful condition of those we seek to lead out of darkness and into His marvelous light. I can say with confidence that Jesus was conscious of our sins, because He came here to die for us and to take upon Himself all the pain and agony that was justifiably due us.

He also proved His worthiness as the ultimate Man in the Middle by showing us when He came to earth that He was compassionate toward our sinful condition.

2. HE WAS COMPASSIONATE TOWARD OUR SINFUL CONDITION.

Jesus came here to forgive us. He knew we were guilty, and He knew how desperately we needed Him. He did not wait for us to come to Him. We were too blinded by sin to even know where to begin our search for Him. We did not know how much we needed Him, and we did not know where to look to find help for what seemed to be a hopeless condition. Jesus came to earth with a heart filled with love and forgiveness.

One of my favorite verses in the Bible is Romans 5:8 "But God demonstrates His own love toward us, in that while we were still sinners, Christ died for us." He did not place a set of moral demands before us to serve as prerequisites for salvation. He died for us while we were still in our sins. This is the epitome of inexplicable love and compassion. He did not force us to pass a test or fill out an application for salvation. He only required us to acknowledge we were sinners, repent of our sins, and by faith believe in what He did for us at Calvary more than two thousand years ago. Our choir sings a song whose title bespeaks of God's compassionate relationship toward fallen humankind: "There Is No Greater Love." His life was not taken from Him, He freely offered Himself as the perfect sacrifice. Even while hanging on the cross, He postponed His death to hear and answer the plea of a guilty sinner who asked the Lord to remember him when He came into His kingdom. Jesus said to him, "Assuredly, I say to you, today you will be with Me in Paradise" (Luke 23:43).

Initially, this verse posed a problem for me. Jesus was in the grave for three days, then He remained here on earth for an additional forty days after His resurrection. I wondered how the thief could be with Him in Paradise on "this day." Then the Holy Spirit reminded me of the fact that Jesus is all God and all man. The spiritual, God part of Jesus ascended back to heaven immediately, and the bodily part of Jesus went back forty-three days later. This thief was really a part of the welcoming committee when Jesus returned home to the right hand of His Father. What amazing love that is!

Now, finally, Jesus came to earth conscious of our sinful condition, compassionate toward our sinful condition, and as the only cure for our sinful condition.

3. CURE FOR OUR SINFUL CONDITION

No one was able to do for us what He did for us. We were on our way to hell without His intervention. This word *intervention* reminds me of a television program I watch occasionally about people with serious addictions. The premise behind the program is to show how the addictions are ruining the lives of people as they are being followed by television cameras. Then the family of the person intervenes, and together they attempt to persuade the addict to seek treatment.

The intervention on television is done by a group of people, but when God intervened for us, He did not have to use a group of people. He only used one person: His only begotten Son, Jesus Christ. He died for us, yes, He did die! But He did not stay dead. (The grammar is poor, but you get the message.) Early one Sunday morning God raised Him from the grave with all power—power to encourage your heart, power to develop your ministry, power to bring change to your life, and power to use you beyond your personal limitations. He is the only cure for our sins, and the prescription has been written in blood, paid in full, and never needs to be repeated.

Walk in your victory and know you are guarded and guided by the ultimate, marvelous Man in the Middle, Jesus Christ.

A WORD FOR PASTORS AND LEADERS

Keep your church and leadership ministries focused on the ultimate Man in the Middle and you will discover He has never taken His eyes off you.

Let Him speak to you, you speak from Him, and watch God do the rest.

And I, if I am lifted up from the earth,
will draw all peoples to Myself.
JOHN 12:32